PROCLAMATION:

**Aids for Interpreting the
Lessons of the Church Year**

PENTECOST 1

SERIES C

Ronald E. Sleeth
and
John R. Donahue

FORTRESS PRESS   Philadelphia, Pennsylvania

Library of Congress Catalog Card Number 73-88347

ISBN 0-8006-4056-X

Second printing 1974

4459E74   Printed in U.S.A.   1-4056

General Preface

Proclamation: Aids for Interpreting the Lessons of the Church Year is a series of twenty-five books designed to help clergymen carry out their preaching ministry. It offers exegetical interpretations of the lessons for each Sunday and many of the festivals of the church year, plus homiletical ideas and insights.

The basic thrust of the series is ecumenical. In recent years the Episcopal church, the Roman Catholic church, the United Church of Christ, and the Lutheran and Presbyterian churches have adopted lectionaries that are based on a common three-year system of lessons for the Sundays and festivals of the church year. *Proclamation* grows out of this development, and authors have been chosen from all of these traditions. Some of the contributors are parish pastors; others are teachers, both of biblical interpretation and of homiletics. Ecumenical interchange has been encouraged by putting two persons from different traditions to work on a single volume, one with the primary responsibility for exegesis and the other for homiletical interpretation.

Despite the high percentage of agreement between the traditions, both in the festivals that are celebrated and the lessons that are appointed to be read on a given day, there are still areas of divergence. Frequently the authors of individual volumes have tried to take into account the various textual traditions, but in some cases this has proved to be impossible; in such cases we have felt constrained to limit the material to the Lutheran readings.

The preacher who is looking for "canned sermons" in these books will be disappointed. These books are one step removed from the pulpit: they explain what the lessons are saying and suggest ways of relating this biblical message to the contemporary situation. As such they are springboards for creative thought as well as for faithful proclamation of the word.

This volume of *Proclamation* has been prepared by Ronald E. Sleeth and John R. Donahue. Professor Sleeth is Professor of Preaching, Perkins School of Theology, Southern Methodist University, Dallas, Tex. He previously taught at Garrett Theological Seminary, Evanston, Ill., and The Divinity School, Vanderbilt University, Nashville, Tenn. In 1972 he was president of the American Academy of Homiletics and during the current academic year is Preacher to the University, Southern Methodist Univer-

iv   *General Preface*

sity, Dallas, Tex. Father Donahue received his Ph.D. in 1972 from the University of Chicago. He is a member of the Society of Jesus and taught at Woodstock College in New York City until the spring of 1973. He is now Professor of New Testament, The Divinity School, Vanderbilt University, Nashville, Tenn.

Introduction

And we thank God constantly for this, that when you received the word
of God which you heard from us, you accepted it not as the work of
man, but as what it really is, the word of God, which is at work in you
believers (1 Thess. 2:13).

In proclaiming the word of God today, the contemporary preacher is
conscious, no less than Paul, that the word has come to him. He stands
as a servant and hearer of the word. He also must hear the hearers of
the word, listen to the listeners—the people of God, and attempt to
make the word of God come alive at every level of their lives. The
present volume is a contribution to this task.

In the exegetical section the aim has been to show what the text *said*
to its original hearers. The exegesis attempts to be as complete and
expansive as possible by listing cross references and allusions for further
study. The homiletical section attempts to show what the text *says*
to its hearers today. Certain themes are suggested though there is no
attempt to develop sermons for the preacher. Also, the exposition does
not limit itself to the exegesis at all points. At times the thematic unity
of the three readings will be unfolded; in other instances unity will not
be forced upon the scripture passages.

It is hoped that the book as a whole will provide both material and
a method for the modern-day preacher who is committed to proclaiming
the gospel as "a workman who has no need to be ashamed, rightly
handling the word of truth" (2 Tim. 2:15).

In preparation of the work the various translations of the Bible with
their notes, such as The Oxford Annotated Bible, The New English
Bible (NEB), The New American Bible (NAB), and The Jerusalem Bible
(JB) have been consulted. The one volume commentaries such as
Peake's Commentary on the Bible, edited by M. Black and H. H.
Rowley (London: Thos. Nelson, 1962), and the *Jerome Biblical Com-
mentary,* edited by R. E. Brown, J. A. Fitzmyer, and R. Murphy
(Englewood Cliffs, N.J.: Prentice Hall, 1968), have been especially help-
ful. To the authors of the essays and commentaries in these works, we
owe a debt of gratitude.

Ronald E. Sleeth
John R. Donahue

Table of Contents

General Preface   iii

Introduction   v

The Day of Pentecost   1

The Holy Trinity, The First Sunday after Pentecost   8

The Second Sunday after Pentecost   13

The Third Sunday after Pentecost   19

The Fourth Sunday after Pentecost   25

The Fifth Sunday after Pentecost   31

The Sixth Sunday after Pentecost   36

The Seventh Sunday after Pentecost   42

The Eighth Sunday after Pentecost   48

The Ninth Sunday after Pentecost   53

The Day of Pentecost

Lutheran	Roman Catholic	Episcopal	Presbyterian and UCC
Gen. 11:1-9	Acts 2:1-11	Acts 2:1-11	Isa. 65:17-25
Acts 2:1-21	1 Cor. 12:3b-7, 12-13	1 Cor. 12:4-13	Acts 2:1-13
John 15:26-27; 16:4b-11	John 20:19-23	John 20:19-23	John 14:25-31

EXEGESIS

Pentecost has often been called "the birthday of the Universal Church." It marks the gift of the Holy Spirit to the small band of believers which set them aflame and sent them out to spread the gospel to the ends of the earth. The preacher seeking an overarching theme in the three lessons will find it essentially in the motif of the original unity of mankind and the disunity associated with the building of the Tower of Babel (First Lesson), the unity brought about in Christ who returns to the Father (Gospel), and the gift of the Holy Spirit to the early witnesses turning them into the Christian church (Acts 2).

First Lesson: Gen. 11:1-9. In form this story is an etiological legend which roots the diversity of language and peoples in an early rebellion. The narrative concludes that part of Genesis traditionally called "the primeval history." This history begins with God's plan of creation and moves tragically through the alienation of man from God and from fellow man (the sin of Adam, of his children, and of his descendants). The nucleus of the present story is that men, still undivided, want to build a tower so they can make a name for themselves. As the story unfolds Yahweh sees in this a form of pride and confuses the language of man.

Thus, the story serves as a conclusion to the spread of sin through man's early history. It also serves as a prelude to the beginning of saving history with the call of Abraham (Genesis 12 ff.) and the forming of a people whom Yahweh himself will name. The narrative has a point of contact with the Pentecost narration (cf. Gen. 11:7 and Acts 2:6 where the same Greek verb, *synchynnō*, is used). In Acts the barrier of confused language is broken as a prelude to a new period of God's action in history and the forming of a new people.

Second Lesson: Acts 2:1-21. In the Lucan account of Pentecost, of initial importance is the setting of the event *in Jerusalem.* Luke's Gospel

1

begins in the temple of Jerusalem (1:5 ff.) and ends there (24:52). Luke locates the last temptation of Jesus in Jerusalem (Luke 4:9–12) and much of the ministry of Jesus is subsumed under the journey where Jesus goes before his disciples toward Jerusalem (Luke 9:51–19:28). In Acts the community begins at Jerusalem (1:4 ff.) which, as for Jesus, is a place of suffering; and trial (Acts 4:3 ff.; 5:18 ff.; 6–7; 8:1). Paul returns to Jerusalem after his conversion (Acts 9:26; 22:17; 26:20) and his final "trial" begins in Jerusalem (Acts 22). By the motif of Jerusalem Luke links the fate of the Christian community with that of Jesus, but in place of a journey toward Jerusalem, the church moves outward from Jerusalem (Acts 1:8) to become the New Israel (cf. Pentecost 7: exegesis of the First Lesson and the discussion of "Symbolic Jerusalem" in the homiletical interpretation).

The narrative, structured around the description of the event (2:1–4), the reaction to the event (2:5–13), and Peter's speech (2:13–40), begins with the notation that the day of Pentecost *had come.* Literally this should be translated "was fulfilled"; Luke uses the same concept to designate two previous critical stages of salvation history: the birth of Jesus (Luke 2:6) and the beginning of the journey to Jerusalem (Luke 9:51). The sound of the mighty wind and the fire are familiar OT images of theophanies (Isa. 66:15 ff.; 1 Kings 19:11 ff.), and in Exod. 19:18 ff. the Lord descends on Sinai "in fire." The scene is also a fulfillment of Luke 3:16, "He will baptize you with the Holy Spirit and fire."

The disciples are "filled with the Holy Spirit." In Luke's theology the Spirit plays a crucial role. John (Luke 1:15), Elizabeth (Luke 1:41), Zachary (Luke 1:67), and Jesus (Luke 4:1) are all filled with the Holy Spirit prior to important events. The giving of the Spirit in Acts 2:4 is in anticipation of the role of the Spirit in Acts. The Spirit instructs the early missionaries (8:29; 10:19 ff.; 11:12; 13:2; 19:21; 21:11); it is the impetus for the proclamation of the Christian message (4:8, 31; 6:10; 11:24) and for conversion (2:38; 8:15 ff.; 10:44 ff.; 11:15; 19:2 ff.). It gives strength to endure persecution (4:29 ff.; 9:16 ff.; 13:52), and is the guiding force in Paul's activity (13:4 ff.; 20:22 ff.; 21:4, 11).

The immediate reaction to the gift of the Spirit is ecstatic speaking within the community (2:4*b*; cf. Acts 10:46; 1 Cor. 12:10; 14:2) and numinous wonder from those outside the community (2:6–7; cf. 1 Cor. 14:22 ff.). Those outside the community hear and understand this event as a sign of the inauguration of the mission to all the world which overcomes the confusion of tongues (Gen. 11:1–9). The note that the first hearers were Jews, "devout men from every nation under the heavens," while emphasizing the universality of the church's mission, also stresses the initial mission to the Jews (cf. Paul's practice of preaching first in synagogues, Acts 13:5; 14:1; 17:1; 18:4), and necessitates in Acts a second "Pentecost of the Gentiles" (Acts 10:44, the Holy Spirit is poured out on Gentiles; 10:46, they speak in tongues). The catalogue of nations (vv. 9–11) moves from East to West, anticipating both the universality and the direction of the church's mission.

The long speech of Peter (the first of the great "missionary speeches" of Acts [cf. 3:11–26; 4:8–12; 5:29–32; 10:34–43; 13:16–41]) begins with an initial defense of the Pentecost event in terms of the fulfillment of the prophecy of Joel (2:28–32). In Joel this is a description of the Day of the Lord, a day of the eschatological outpouring of the Spirit, a day of salvation for those faithful to Yahweh, and, at the same time, a day of judgment and the vindication of God's righteousness (cf. Amos 5:18–20; Isa. 2:10 ff.; Zeph. 1:14 ff.).

The Pentecost event as narrated by Luke is foundational for the future of the church, links the witness of the church to the ministry of Jesus, and anticipates the role of the Spirit in the church.

Gospel: John 15:26–27; 16:4b–11. A major theme running through the final discourses of Jesus in John's Gospel (13:31–17:26) is that Jesus' journey to death is his way to the Father (cf. 14:3; 16:17, 28). A disciple must be prepared to follow this way, but Jesus' departure does not mean complete separation for he goes to prepare for them (14:2 ff.), to intercede for them (16:23), and they will enjoy his presence, though in another fashion, through the presence of the Paraclete (14:16, 26; 15:26; 16:7)—called also the Spirit of truth (14:17; 15:26; 16:13) and the Holy Spirit (14:26). In the Gospel for today, immediately after speaking of the world's opposition in 15:18–25, Jesus promises the Paraclete (Counselor) who will bear witness to Jesus as the disciples are called to do (15:25–27), and convict the world (16:8–11).

The meaning of the term "Paraclete," also translated as "Counselor," "Advocate," or "Helper," is disputed. It has the forensic sense of defense lawyer, but is used also in the wider context of one who appears on another's behalf, a mediator, an intercessor, or a helper. In 1 John 2:1, Jesus is called a Paraclete, so the Spirit in John 14:16 is "another Paraclete." In the Gospel of John the Paraclete comes forth from the Father (15:26) as did Jesus (5:43). The Paraclete is the Spirit of truth (14:17); Jesus is *the truth* (14:6). The Paraclete teaches and guides the disciples (14:26; 16:13) as did Jesus (6:59; 7:14, 18; 8:20). The Paraclete (15:26) and Jesus (8:14) both give witness, and the world cannot accept the Paraclete (14:17) as evil men did not accept Jesus (5:43; 12:48). Therefore the Paraclete performs in the church the function Jesus performed in his ministry. The Spirit is the presence of the absent Jesus who operates in the Christian proclamation, confirms and instructs disciples, and judges the world.

In 16:8–11 a threefold indictment of the world is effected by the Paraclete. It should be noted that "world" in John is not the arena of man's everyday activity, but rather a symbol of unbelief and opposition to God's revelation. The Paraclete will convict the world of the sin of unbelief (cf. 15:21–23); of righteousness because the world does not recognize true righteousness in the cross and resurrection of Jesus; and of judgment because by the death of Christ the powers of the world are judged. Thus, the Spirit in John functions much like the power of the gospel does for Paul. (Cf. Rom. 1:18 ff., conviction of sin; Rom. 4:25, the true righteousness; Gal. 4:3 ff., the victory over the powers of the world.) In his emphasis on the role of the Spirit in the church, more than Luke, John stresses the crisis which the presence of the Spirit brings to men's lives.

HOMILETICAL INTERPRETATION

First Lesson. The Genesis story is a fascinating saga and lends itself to all kinds of homiletical treatment for Pentecost. The NEB begins the passage in almost fairy-tale fashion, perhaps reflecting the Eden-like quality of unity before Babel: "Once upon a time." It is an arresting beginning for a story which tells of man's attempt to usurp God's prerogatives and the punishment that follows. This motif, along with the making and breaking of covenants, is a recurring one in the biblical drama of salvation and is repeated in a hundred different ways all through the biblical drama of history.

One of the preeminent themes in the Genesis passage is the persistent one of *idolatry.* V. 4 indicates this concept: 1. "Come, let us build *ourselves* a city. . . ." (RSV). Right off one sees the impending disaster with the self-centered motivation for building. The psalmist reminds us that, "Unless the Lord builds the house those who build it labor in vain" (Psalm 127). The ancient yet modern theme of pride is the essence of man's struggle with righteousness. This sin which is within the heart of man is as ancient as the once-upon-a-time of Genesis and as current as the now-ness of the daily newspaper. 2. ". . . a tower with its top in the sky. . . ." (NAB). The first skyscraper was built upon presumption, to reach the heavens. This is the greatest idolatry, to encroach upon God's sovereignty. It had happened before with Adam in Gen. 3:22. His sin in eating the apple was not the attempt to gain knowledge, but to transgress into God's realm. While with Adam it was an individual idolatry, here we move from *man* to *men*. Even men in society are tempted in every generation to overshoot their status as dependent beings.

Another interesting theme in the Genesis verses is the ironic quality of ambition and punishment. The builders' rationalization for the tower was to make a name for themselves, ". . . lest we be scattered abroad upon the face of the whole earth" (RSV). Their punishment was precisely that: "So the Lord scattered them abroad from there over the face of all the earth . . ." (v. 8). Their desires crumbled like dust and the very thing they feared became their punishment. Their desires were good, but ironically their idolatry canceled their desires. The imaginative preacher can easily see the timelessness of that theme.

Close to this theme is another aspect of the nature of the punishment. The Lord confused their speech—made them babblers. He made them uncommunicative. Is there any more contemporary punishment for men's sins—their lack of faithfulness, their idolatry—than the inability to communicate? From the family to politics to international relations, the lack of unity has made babblers of us all. For the Christian, the unity that brings communication alive again is the faithful covenant relation to the Lord.

Second Lesson. The key passage for the Pentecost experience comes from Acts 2. Here is the historical drama of the Spirit coming upon the disciples. It is significant that the unity that came in Christ found them of *one* accord and in *one* place. There was a *togetherness* in Christ that contrasts significantly with the Tower of Babel dispersion, precisely because the symbol of unity was the Christ event, not the disciples' selfish desires. Even the diversity of tongues to which they gave utterance and which could be understood by foreigners contrasts sharply with the babbling in Genesis because of the unity brought about by the Holy Spirit. What a saga could be written—or preached— on the events between "Once upon a time" (NEB) in Genesis to the "all together in one place" in this lesson. It is a story of salvation— a veritable drama of redemption.

The preacher will notice two emphases here which will prove invaluable in dealing with Pentecost Sunday. The first, of course, is the gift of *glossolalia*—speaking in tongues. Two temptations should be avoided by the preacher: 1) that the speaking of tongues can be ignored in this passage—it was certainly a common experience in the early church (cf. 1 Cor. 12:4–14); 2) that *glossolalia* is the central or only emphasis of the Pentecost experience.

We now have a rekindling of interest in the phenomenon of speaking in tongues not only in the Pentecostal sects, but in the traditional churches as well. One should not minimize this manifestation of the Spirit. However, the preacher needs to remember two things about *glossolalia*: it was the *Spirit* that gave them the *gift* of speech. That is, the speaking in tongues is not a self-induced experience nor a reason for pride. It is a gift of God. Both the nature of the gift and the coherence with the total God-like life should be in our minds as tests for the authenticity of tongue-speaking. The other word of caution is that the phenomenon must be seen alongside of St. Paul's strictures in 1 Corinthians 14. Although the whole chapter is a backdrop for speculating on tongue-speaking, vv. 4–6 are especially helpful in distinguishing between the language of ecstasy, which is personal, and prophecy, which builds up the community.

The second emphasis in this lesson is not on speaking in tongues at all. The apostles because of the unity in Christ speak a universal language. The unity lost at Babel is here restored. In Genesis unity had been sought through man's own efforts. In Acts it is a gift from God. This experience symbolizes the collective nature of the group and its worldwide mission. In John the Spirit was given to the apostles by Jesus; at Pentecost it became a "public charisma for the Church" (cf. notes in NAB). No longer would the apostles be private witnesses; their band would move out in mission as a witnessing church.

Peter's sermon, only part of which is included in this pericope, is significant for two reasons: 1) it tells us that NT preaching followed a distinct pattern of relating Jesus to the prophets, telling again of the mighty acts done by God in him, his crucifixion at their hands, his triumph over death in the resurrection, the lordship of Christ, the call to repentance, baptism, the forgiveness of sins, and the reception of the Holy Spirit. This was the heart of their proclamation; indeed, telling this story was preaching the gospel itself. 2) Even though it would be too much to claim that this should be an exact paradigm for our preaching today, it is not too much to say that the heart of a sermon is the kerygmatic proclamation of what God has done and continues to do in Christ Jesus.

Gospel. The Gospel lesson follows easily from the OT passage, for in contrast to the dispersion of the Tower of Babel, Christ brings unity. For the Christian, it is clear that Jesus Christ is the focus of the faith which unites us all with the Father.

The theological import of the Gospel pericope is obvious. John indicates Jesus' place in the Trinity and his relationship to the Holy

Spirit. Indeed, Jesus himself will send the Advocate, demonstrating his claim to be the Son of God (cf. notes in JB).

Beyond the unity of Jesus and the nature of the Trinity, preaching on the Holy Spirit itself evokes a challenge. Many feel it is one of the least clear of all the Christian affirmations. It seems difficult to concretize. Thus, it goes all the way from an abstract theological doctrine to a ghostly, "spooky" concept which is subjective and centered on feelings of the Spirit. This passage gives some indication, however, of interesting homiletical approaches. First, it is clear that the Spirit is *truth*. It is not simply a subjective spiritual experience; it is validated by the truth that issues transcendently—from the Father himself. Second, there are two aspects to the work of the Spirit: (a) it will bear witness of itself. When Jesus returns to the Father, the Spirit will come to continue to bear witness to the work of Jesus Christ. (b) The disciples also are to witness. They have the mandate to continue their witness because they have been with him from the beginning. Though the witness is not entirely different, the witnessing will have a varying function. The Advocate will come and validate one's faith, but the disciples' witness will be equally valid as they testify to the work of the Advocate. The distinction might even be made between the interior witness of the Paraclete and the external witness of the disciples—and by extension, the church itself (cf. the NAB notes on John 15:27). The importance of the disciples' witness—and the church's—is evidenced in the post-resurrection appearance recorded in John 20:19–23. Jesus equated the disciples' role with his own, signifying that the church is the body of Christ. He blessed them, giving the Holy Spirit, and the power to forgive sins.

Apart from the dual nature of the work of the Holy Spirit, another fruitful avenue of approach for the preacher is the variety of names given for the Holy Spirit itself. Comforter, Counselor, Advocate, Spirit of Truth, Divine Helper, Paraclete, and Helper. Work on one or more of these synonyms can lead to an arresting sermon on the Holy Spirit through the elaboration of an interesting term. Take *helper*, for example, and see that both in terms of personal witness and in the life of the church. As a beginning, ask the question: How can or does the church act as *helper*? Worship, prayer, preaching, human concern, mutual support, social outreach?

The Holy Trinity,
The First Sunday after Pentecost

Lutheran	Roman Catholic	Episcopal	Presbyterian and UCC
Num. 6:22–27	Prov. 8:22–31	Num. 6:22–27	Prov. 8:22–31
Rom. 5:1–5	Rom. 5:1–5	Rom. 8:12–17	1 Pet. 1:1–9
John 16:12–15	John 16:12–15	John 14:8–17	John 20:19–23

EXEGESIS

First Lesson: Num. 6:22–27. These verses contain the famous "priestly blessing," the use of which is described in Sir. 50:20 ff. and which was pronounced at the morning sacrifice in the temple. "The Lord bless you": Blessing in the OT is at the same time a communication of life (Gen. 1:22, 28; 5:2) and a promise of fidelity (Gen. 12:2–3). "And keep you": Yahweh is often called the keeper or watcher of Israel and Psalm 121 represents an extended and beautiful commentary on "he who keeps Israel [who] will neither slumber nor sleep." "The Lord make his face shine upon you": The "shining of the face" is either a paraphrase for "smile" or a metaphor taken from the dawning of a new day. In the OT there is a clear connection between the "shining of the face" and salvation—Ps. 80:3, 7, 19, "Let thy face shine, that we may be saved" (cf. also Ps. 31:16; 67:1; Dan. 9:17). "And be gracious to you": The verb "be gracious or show favor" (Hebrew, *hanan*; Greek, *charis*, "grace," or *eleos*, "mercy") appears most often in the context of finding favor in God's eyes. God shows favor to man by delivering him from distress (Pss. 4:1; 6:2; 9:13; 25:16; 26:11; 27:7). When used of men the verb describes an attitude one should adopt in respect to the needy, the poor, and those who are in any distress. "The Lord lift up his countenance": In Job 11:15 this is a sign of acceptance by God and in Ps. 4:6–7, a sign of joy. "And give you peace": Peace is virtually a one word symbol for total happiness in the OT. It connotes health, wholeness, prosperity, harmony between man and nature, between man and God, and between man and his brother.

In older exegesis this blessing was seen as "Trinitarian" in the threefold use of *Lord,* but this represents an accommodation of the OT to the New. The connection with today's feast is rather in the fullness of blessings which comes upon man when he finds favor with God (cf. Rom. 5:1–5, where peace and grace are also mentioned).

Second Lesson: Rom. 5:1–5. Having established in Romans 1–4 that the justification of man by God takes place through faith in Jesus Christ,

Paul begins to describe the Christian experience of justification. These verses comprise one of a series of "triadic" texts in Paul (Rom. 8:14–17; 15:30; 1 Cor. 2:7–16; 6:11; 2 Cor. 1:21–22) where the Father, Son, and Spirit function in the economy of salvation. Here Paul speaks of the past—justification through faith; of the present—joy amid trials made possible by the gift of the Spirit; and of the future—hope for sharing in the glory of God.

"We have peace with God": Other manuscripts read "let us have peace with God." Paul emphasizes that by being justified the right relation of man to God has been established (Rom. 14:17; 15:13; Eph. 2:14–15, Christ, our peace). "We rejoice in our hope of sharing the glory of God . . . we rejoice in our sufferings" (cf. Pentecost 7 and 9: exegesis of Second Lesson and homiletical interpretation). Paul posits a double rejoicing here—in hope and in suffering. "Rejoice" is too weak to convey Paul's intention. The verb literally means "boast" and Paul often contrasts the Christian's boast which is the paradox of joy amid suffering and weakness with the false boasting of his opponents (1 Cor. 1:29, 31; 3:21; 4:7; 2 Cor. 10:13–18; 12:1–10). "In our sufferings": The sufferings in Paul are twofold (a) anything which would separate man from God (Rom. 8:35; 1 Cor. 4:11–12; 7:26–32), and (b) the tribulations which characterize the final age before the return of the Lord (1 Thess. 1:6; 3:3; 2 Thess. 1:6, cf. Mark 13:19, 24; Matt. 24:9, 29). "Character produces hope": The translation "character" runs the risk of giving the impression that Paul is talking about the psychological role of suffering. More accurate translations would be "tested virtue" (NAB) or "proof that we have stood the test" (NEB). The point here is that the testing is an eschatological trial which for the Christian should increase his hope. In the NT hope involves three elements: (a) trust, (b) expectation of the future, and (c) patient waiting. "Hope does not disappoint us": Paul roots the hope in the presence of God's love which is poured (cf. Acts 2:17) into our hearts through the Spirit. It is important to realize that Paul continually emphasizes the human or experiential counterpart to God's saving action. This experience is the paradox of faith, of strength in weakness, of joy amid tribulation—the anthropological counterpart to the mystery of the cross and resurrection.

Gospel: John 16:12–15. This section continues last Sunday's Gospel, the discourse of Jesus on his departure and the coming of the Paraclete. In 16:8–11 the role of the Paraclete in indicting the world was stressed; here his role as instructor is developed.

"The Spirit of truth" is a title which, along with "Holy Spirit" (14:26), is given the Paraclete. "He will guide you into all truth": The imagery

In the NT, Saul became Paul after the Damascus road experience. A
fruitful line of approach would be to ask what difference it makes to
wear the name "Christian." How does that denote an essential change
of being? What difference does it make to belong to the body of Christ
and be God's person?

Second Lesson. Nothing is more important to St. Paul than the concept of justification by faith. It is indeed pivotal for all Christians. It
has become a shibboleth for Protestant Christians since the Reformation.
In truth, it is as old as the Christian faith itself and is the cornerstone
of the church's theology—not just Pauline theology. Paul, however, is
possessed by this concept. He keeps referring to it as if it were an
overwhelming idea. The "therefore" that begins the passage indicates
that he has been dealing with the mind-shattering affirmation that we
rely utterly upon God and not upon ourselves for our salvation
(Romans 1–4).

The basic idea of the gift of God's love to us through Jesus Christ is
replete with preaching possibilities. The doctrinal theme of *justification*
can be dealt with as a theme, though doctrinal preaching per se
always risks the temptation of abstractness. More fruitful would be to
take some aspect of justification and deal with that. For example, take
God's gift of love irrespective of whether we deserve it. Such a belief
is basic to Christian faith, yet incredible. Somehow we cannot believe
that God's love is so overpowering that it accepts the unacceptable.
We want to believe we must do something to earn or deserve his love,
yet Paul assures us that it is our faith, not our works, which gives us
peace with God. On the human level such love is equally baffling. We
all know people who cannot receive gifts. A gift from a friend immediately brings one in return. A dinner invitation is promptly returned.
How difficult it is for us to receive something freely given! The gift of
love in marriage is appropriate too. The love that binds husband and
wife together is one that accepts even the unacceptable traits of the
other. If this kind of love is difficult for us to understand on the human
level, then it is no wonder that we have difficulty in seeing the nature
of divine love which wipes away man's guilt and justifies him before
God.

Two other ideas leap out of the exegesis. One is the idea of rejoicing
in suffering. What kind of faith would one envision which enables us
to rejoice (or boast) in suffering? This faith is not only the kind which
enabled the early Christians to withstand the trials and persecutions
as they waited for the early return of their Lord. It is also the faith that
enables modern-day Christians to undergo trials with joy, if we remem-

ber that trials are not only persecutions but anything which separates men from God. The second idea is the one of *hope.* The exegesis itself suggests three elements which push the preacher's mind into a creative area. How can (a) trust, (b) expectation of the future, and (c) patient waiting be translated into our specific situation as a Christian community?

Gospel. As the exegesis indicates, the Gospel continues the sixteenth chapter discourse on the Spirit. Much of the exposition from last Sunday would pertain to today's lesson. It was suggested then that the various names for the Holy Spirit provide the basis for an interesting sermon. The exegesis for today lifts up *instructor* as the key aspect of the Paraclete's work in this passage. The Holy Spirit as instructor— the Spirit of truth—provides a framework for relating the Holy Spirit to specific content of the Christian faith. It also reinforces the earlier idea in the homiletical interpretation that one or more of the terms used for the Spirit might not only be the basis for a specific sermon, but might indeed furnish the background for a series of sermons on the nature and work of the Holy Spirit.

The trinitarian emphasis is also repeated in this passage. Jesus is talking about the Spirit which will be coming. Since Jesus relates himself to the Father and the Holy Spirit here, the trinitarian formula is clearly established. The preacher needs to be careful with this powerful doctrine. This is not tritheism, but the *one* work of God in Christ continued in the coming of the Paraclete. "There are not three revelations but one" (JB).

The Second Sunday after Pentecost

Lutheran	Roman Catholic	Episcopal	Presbyterian and UCC
1 Kings 8:41–43	1 Kings 8:41–43	1 Kings 8:41–43	1 Kings 8:41–43
Gal. 1:1–10	Gal. 1:1–2, 6–10	Gal. 1:1–10	Gal. 1:1–10
Luke 7:1–10	Luke 7:1–10	Luke 7:1–10	Luke 7:1–10

EXEGESIS

First Lesson: 1 Kings 8:41–43. Today's lesson is from the prayer of Solomon (1 Kings 8:23–53) as he dedicates the first temple. Though set in this context, the language and spirit of the prayer mirror the

larger context of the Deuteronomic history (Deuteronomy–2 Kings) which
reached its final form after the Babylonian exile (c. 550 B.C.). A major
motif of this history is a message of faith and encouragement to those
returning from exile that the promise to David, "your house and
your kingdom shall be made sure for ever before me" (2 Sam. 7:16),
will be fulfilled and that the Lord will be present in the temple and
the royal city, Jerusalem. Thus, the hopes of the returning community
for the second temple are put on the lips of Solomon as he dedicates
the first.

Solomon prays (vv. 41–43) that "all the peoples of the earth may know
thy name and fear thee." This universalistic hope characterizes exilic
and postexilic literature (e.g., Isaiah 40–55; Jonah; Zech. 8:20–23).
"When a foreigner comes" (v. 41): The foreigner is not the "resident alien"
whose rights in Israel were determined by law (Num. 15:14 ff.), but
one completely outside Israel's influence. "For thy name's sake" (v. 41):
The foreigner comes attracted initially by the name of Israel's God. In
the OT, "name" means the revealed nature and character of God (cf.
Deut. 12:5-21; 1 Kings 8:27–30; cf. homiletical interpretation for the
Holy Trinity, Pentecost 1). By terms like "name," "glory," and "face"
Israel expressed both the nearness and distance of God. The Lord is
not confined to the temple, but his saving presence is there. "And thy
mighty hand and outstretched arm" (v. 42): The mighty hand and
outstretched arm are classic terms to describe the deliverance from
slavery in Egypt (cf. Exod. 3:19; 6:1, 6; 13:3, 9, 16; 15:6, 12; Deut.
4:34; 6:21; 7:19; 9:29). Therefore the second reason the foreigner comes
is that he hears of the saving Lord of the Exodus liberation. "In order
that all the peoples of the earth may know thy name and fear thee"
(v. 43): The coming of the foreigner is a prelude to the rule of Israel's
Lord over all nations. The *fear* of the Lord is not a psychological
fright, but the awe man experiences in the face of the holy (cf.
Exod. 3:6).

The connection of the lesson with the Gospel is clear. In both cases
a foreigner comes, attracted by the presence and saving power of the
Lord.

Second Lesson: Gal. 1:1–10. For the following six Sundays the epistles
are from Galatians, often called the Magna Charta of Christian freedom
and which Luther called "my epistle to which I am betrothed." In this
letter Paul hammers out, in conflict with opponents, the major themes
of his "gospel" which receive extended and reflected treatment in
Romans. (Gal. 2:15–21 is virtually an outline of Romans 1–8.) The letter
is polemical in tone—the substitution of "I am astonished" (1:6) for the

usual thanksgiving; reference to those who "pervert the gospel of Christ" (1:7); and characterization of the Galatians as "foolish" (3:1). The precise identity of the opponents is unclear. On the one hand, they appear to be "Judaizers" who attack Paul's right to be an apostle (1:11–16) and who want to force Paul's converts to observe the Jewish law (2:12–3:5; 4:9–10; 5:2). On the other hand, Paul criticizes a tendency toward misuse of freedom by them (5:13 ff.). Whether the opponents were Judaizers or local sectarian groups, tinged with Gnosticism, is less important than the realization that Paul expresses his strongest and most profound reflection on the meaning of the Christ event in living dialogue with real problems facing his community.

The letter is divided into an introduction (1:1–9), a defense by Paul of his gospel of justification by faith (1:10–2:21), a scriptural proof that in God's plan faith, not the law, saves man (3:1–4:31), the consequences of this justification in the freedom of the Christian (5:1–6:10), and a conclusion (6:11–18; cf. Fitzmyer, *Jerome Biblical Commentary*, II, 238).

Paul introduces Galatians, 1 Corinthians, 2 Corinthians, and Colossians by designating himself an apostle, but only here adds the qualification, "not from men or through man." In the language of this period an "apostle" is "one sent out," a representative of a higher power with full authority to perform a definite task (legal, prophetic, or missionary). "But through Jesus Christ and God the Father": Paul roots his gospel and his right to proclaim it in the power of the risen Christ (Gal. 1:12; 1 Cor. 15:8). "Grace and peace" (v. 3): The standard Pauline formula for the goods of the messianic age (cf. Gal. 6:15–16; cf. Trinity, First Lesson and Pentecost 7, Gospel). "Who gave himself" (v. 4): This sounds the dominant theme of the letter—salvation through the self-giving or emptying of Jesus (cf. Gal. 2:20; Phil. 2:7–8). Though Paul sees himself as a missionary of the risen Christ, he never loses sight of the cross in the saving plan of God (Gal. 6:14).

In the final verses of the introduction (v. 10 is a transitional verse), Paul sets the tone of the whole letter by stating that there is only one authentic ˋgospel and anathematizing anyone (v. 9) who preaches a different gospel. For Paul the gospel is both the act of proclaiming (cf. Phil. 4:15; 2 Cor. 2:12; 8:18), and the content of the proclamation, "the power of God for salvation to everyone who has faith" (Rom. 1:16). For this reason Paul defends both his right to proclaim the gospel and the content of the proclamation.

Gospel: Luke 7:1–10. In both Matthew and Luke mighty works of Jesus (miracles) follow an extended sermon (Matthew 5–7; Luke 6:20–49).

The miracles of the Gospels are signs, no less than the teaching of Jesus, which point to the presence of God and the inauguration of the new age (cf. Luke 4:16–30; Pentecost 3: exegesis of the Gospel and the homiletical interpretation). The healing of the centurion's servant is from the source common to Matthew and Luke (Q) and, though there are considerable variations in the respective narratives—in Luke Jesus never speaks directly to the centurion; Luke omits the harsh saying against the Jews (Matt. 8:11–12)—both evangelists see the high point of the narrative in the saying, "I tell you, not even in Israel have I found such faith" (7:9; Matt. 8:10). The narrative represents a very old tradition and John 4:46–54 (the healing of the official's son) may represent a variation of the same tradition.

"When he heard of Jesus he sent to him elders of the Jews" (v. 3): Like the foreigner of 1 Kings 8:41 ff. the centurion (a Gentile official) "hears" of Jesus. The delegation brings the request for healing; Jesus starts toward the house and a second delegation brings the response of the centurion: "Lord I am not worthy to have you come under my roof." This is not simply a protestation of humility, but a portrayal of the sensitivity of the centurion to Jewish custom. "But say the word and let my servant be healed (v. 7) . . . Not even in Israel have I found such faith" (v. 9): The essence of the narrative is found in these verses. In almost half of the healing miracles of the Gospels there is this conjunction of faith and healing (the paralytic, Mark 2:5; Matt. 9:2; Luke 5:20; the woman who touches Jesus' garment, Mark 5:34; Matt. 9:22; Luke 8:48; Jairus's daughter, Mark 5:36; Luke 8:50; the two blind men, Matt. 9:29; the blind Bartimaeus, Mark 10:52; Luke 18:42; the epileptic boy, Mark 9:24; the daughter of the Canaanite woman, Matt. 15:28; and the ten lepers, Luke 17:19). This conjunction suggests that it is faith which not only draws a person to Jesus, but also gives him wholeness. This faith is a "hearing" (7:3); it is a confident trust in the word of Jesus (7:7), and a grasping after the help of God. It is at the same time the power which liberates man from the powers which enslave him. In this sense the healing of the centurion's servant "at a distance" is a paradigm of faith for all who hear the word of Christ.

HOMILETICAL INTERPRETATION

The theme of this Sunday's lessons is the continuing outreach of the people of God to all men. The Christian community is one which moves out in mission. It is not exclusive, but inclusive. It is not particular, but universal. The scripture passages demonstrate clearly that we do not

being challenged. In Luke 5 when Jesus called Matthew to be a disciple, the Pharisees challenged him for eating and drinking with tax collectors and sinners. Jesus answered, "I have not come to call the righteous, but sinners to repentance." He still does, and the righteous are still upset. The faith of the "outsider," the unbelieving believer, or what Karl Rahner describes as the "anonymous" Christian is a rich vein for Christian preaching proceeding from this passage.

The brief encounter with the soldier also dramatizes the scope of Jesus' *authority* in his ministry. Here the centurion compares his own with Jesus' as a point of contact. Elsewhere in the Gospels Jesus' authority is often recognized by those outside the faith sometimes even before it is recognized by those who were his followers. The woman at the well, healed lepers, men possessed by demons—all testified to the authority of Jesus even though they were outsiders to the community of believers. Another thread in the pericope is the nature of *faith* in regard to the healing of the son. (See exegesis on relation between faith and healing. The preacher might well reflect on the healing power of faith today.) Although we see the faith of an unbeliever in the centurion, we have no indication of any in the child. Jesus' ministry was even to those who either had no faith of their own or depended upon the faith of others to enact their cure. There is something powerfully moving in the grace and love of God in Christ which come even to those who have little or no faith. What a tremendous way to emphasize both God's grace and the inclusive nature of his love.

The Third Sunday after Pentecost

Lutheran	Roman Catholic	Episcopal	Presbyterian and UCC
1 Kings 17:17–24	1 Kings 17:17–24	1 Kings 17:17–24	1 Kings 17:17–24
Gal. 1:11–24	Gal. 1:11–19	Gal. 1:11–19	Gal. 1:11–19
Luke 7:11–17	Luke 7:11–17	Luke 7:11–17	Luke 7:11–17

EXEGESIS

First Lesson: 1 Kings 17:17–24. Today's lesson is from the Elijah cycle (1 Kings 17–19, 21–2 Kings 1) which, along with the Elisha cycle (2 Kings 2:1–8:29), represents very old material (9th–8th cent. B.C.) incorporated into the Deuteronomic history. In these stories many themes which are found in the classical prophets emerge: the prophet as a spokesman of the word of the Lord (1 Kings 17:1); the rejection and persecution of the prophet (1 Kings 18:17); the struggle of the prophet against syncretism and idolatry (1 Kings 17:20–18:46); the concern of the prophet for the helpless (widows) and those who suffer injustice (1 Kings 21); the prophetic complaint and discouragement (1 Kings 19:4 ff.); the wonder working power of the prophet (1 Kings 17:8–24); and the symbolic action of the prophet (1 Kings 17:21; cf. Pentecost 6: exegesis of the First Lesson and the discussion of prophecy in the homiletical interpretation). The figure of Elijah exercises a special influence on later Jewish literature and on the NT, especially because of his "translation" (2 Kings 2:11) and his expected return as forerunner of the day of the Lord (Mal. 4:5).

The resuscitation of the son of the widow of Zarephath exhibits the same structure as the NT miracles: (1) the setting or description of the problem (1 Kings 17:17–20), (2) the miraculous activity (vv. 17–23), and (3) the reaction to this activity (v. 24), usually in the form of praise of God. *The setting:* The woman (17:18) interprets the death of her son as a punishment for sin (cf. John 9:2) which the presence of a man of God brings to light. *The miracle:* The resuscitation is preceded by a prayer. As Lord of life and death, God is pictured as *slaying* the son. Elijah, in a symbolic rite of resuscitation stretches himself over the boy (cf. 2 Kings 4:34, Elisha; Acts 20:10, Paul). This rite symbolizes that the life force is so strong in a man of God (17:18, 24) that it is communicated to the dead youth. The joining of word and symbolic activity in the OT is a standard feature of prophetic activity (e.g. 2 Kings 20:7; Hosea 1–3; Jer. 13:1–2; Ezek. 4:1–5:17) and anticipates the conjunction of word and mighty work in the ministry of Jesus. *The reaction:* The woman confesses that Elijah is a man of God and that the word of his Lord (Yahweh) is true. The miracle confirms the presence of the Lord in the word of the prophet.

Second Lesson: Gal. 1:11–24. Here Paul emphasizes the independence of his gospel by rooting it directly in his conversion experience (1:12) and by stressing that it was only *after* his initial missionary activity that he made his first visit to Jerusalem (1:17).

"It came through a revelation of Jesus Christ" (v. 12): The basic meaning of revelation is to disclose or un-conceal. In the Bible it is used not as the disclosure of supernatural knowledge, but of the realization of the coming of God in an event and in the NT the event of the death and resurrection of Jesus (cf. Rom. 16:25 ff.). When Paul emphasizes the immediacy of the revelation given him, he is not talking about knowing the content of the life and ministry of Jesus (he describes little of this in his letters), nor is he saying that he is independent of the traditions of the churches (cf. 1 Cor. 11:23–25; 15:1–7), but he is stressing that the inner meaning of the Christ event was communicated to him.

Gal. 1:13–17 recounts Paul's conversion. The Lucan accounts of Paul's conversion in Acts (9:3–19; 22:6–16; 26:12–18) and Paul's own version in Galatians and Phil. 3:4–11, while differing in detail, all affirm the status of Paul as persecutor, the sudden, gratuitous, and overwhelming nature of the conversion, and Paul's conviction that he had been given understanding into the mystery of Christ. "When he who had set me apart" (v. 15): Paul links his vocation to a prophetic call (cf. Jer. 1:5, "Before I formed you in the womb I knew you" and Isa. 49:1, "The Lord called me from the womb, from the body of my mother he named my name"). Like the prophets, Paul is the recipient of a theophany and, like them, his mission is not simply to his own people, but to the Gentiles (v. 16). His mission is *to preach him* (v. 16). The verb "preach" is from the same root as the word for "gospel," so Paul's mission is to spread the good news about Jesus.

Gal. 1:18–24 deals with the Jerusalem visit. Paul does not tell us the content of his meeting with Cephas and James. The word for "visit" literally means "make inquiry of," so Paul may have been instructed in the traditions of the Jerusalem church. In vv. 22–24, while affirming that he did not preach in Judea, Paul states that "they glorified God because of me." To give glory is a response to revelation so that Paul states that his conversion had a prophetic effect on the Jerusalem community, and that, implicitly, his apostolate and gospel were recognized as valid.

Gospel: Luke 7:11–17. This is one of the eight miracles which Luke alone narrates (5:1–11; 7:11–17; 7:21; 9:11; 13:10–17; 14:1–6; 17:11–19; 22:51). It also exhibits particular Lucan concerns and motifs: the role of women in Luke's Gospel (cf. Luke 1–2; 7:36–50; 8:1–3; 10:38–42; 11:27–28; 15:8–9; 23:27–31; cf. Pentecost 4 and 9: exegesis of the Gospels and the homiletical interpretation); the mention of compassion, 7:13 (1:78; 10:33; 15:20); the "glorifying" of God, 7:16 (2:20; 13:13; 17:15; 18:43; 23:47); God "visiting" his people, 7:16 (1:68, 78) and the portrayal of Jesus as a model of care and concern. The contacts between this narrative and the Elijah story of the First Lesson are striking: the meeting at the gate of the city (7:12; 1 Kings 17:10); the woman as a widow (7:12; 1 Kings 17:10); the phrase "he gave him to his mother" is exactly the same as the Septuagint version of 1 Kings 17:23;

both narratives conclude with the confession that the wonder worker is a prophet (7:16; 1 Kings 17:24) and that God is manifest in the work.

Such contacts suggest that Luke has used the OT narrative to portray Jesus on the model of a prophet—a concern which permeates his Gospel. Like Hannah, the mother of Samuel, Mary prays a canticle (1 Sam. 2:1–10; Luke 1:46–55). Jesus is to be a light for the revelation of Gentiles (2:32; Isa. 42:6). Unlike Matthew and Mark, Luke places the rejection at Nazareth at the very beginning of Jesus' ministry and makes it into a combination of a prophetic anointing of Jesus (4:18–19) and a story of prophetic rejection (the mention of Elijah and Elisha is explicit only in Luke, 4:25–27). Jesus says, in reference to himself, that a prophet should not perish away from Jerusalem (13:33) and, after the resurrection, the disciples are said to have understood Jesus as a prophet "mighty in deed and word" (24:19). Like the prophets Jesus speaks on behalf of God (6:7, 20–49); he performs symbolic actions and mighty works (the miracles) and speaks in symbolic language (the parables). Other characteristics of Luke's Gospel show the influence of OT prophecy—the concern for outsiders: the widow (7:11 ff.), a Samaritan (10:29–37), the lepers (17:11 ff.), and the emphasis on the message of the covenant qualities of mercy (1:50, 54, 58, 72, 78; 10:37) and grace (*charis*; 2:40; 4:22; 6:32–34).

Thus, in today's Gospel the "sign" quality of the miracles of Jesus is stressed. The miracles are signs not only that the power and presence of God is manifest in Jesus, but signs that the hopes of the Old Covenant are fulfilled in Jesus. In the OT, contact with the "man of God" is life-giving. In today's Gospel, contact with Jesus, the new prophet, is life-giving and evokes the same response of awesome fear and praise of God.

HOMILETICAL INTERPRETATION

The theme of today's lessons could be, "The Authentication of Prophets." Variations on this theme would include the role of the prophet, relation of God's man both to God and his people, vindication of apostleship, and the certification of God's spokesmen. In the case of Elijah, he was acclaimed as a man of God when he brought the widow's son back to life. Paul vindicates his apostleship by relating how a revelation of Jesus Christ turned him from a persecuting zealot to a preacher of the faith by whom men glorify God. When Jesus brought to life the widow's son at Nain, the response was that a great prophet had arisen and God had visited his people.

One of the first homiletical problems the preacher must face is the place of the miraculous in these pericopes. In the cases of Jesus and

Elijah, the miracle seems to authenticate their roles as agents of God. As to Paul, the cataclysmic encounter on the road to Damascus was a "miracle" even though less explicit than the other two. At first reading one may overlook two important aspects of the miraculous in these passages. First, the writers of Scripture made little distinction between natural events and what might be called supernatural ones. A second and more important aspect for preaching, is that in many cases we regard Jesus' miracles as proof of God's activity while the evangelist, writing after the resurrection, would assume Jesus' lordship and would see the miracle simply as a sign that Jesus was the Son of God. In regard to all biblical miracles, the preacher should avoid two extremes: 1. overlooking the miracle by rationalizing it out of the passage, and 2. thinking the miracle is either at the heart of the event described or the only phenomenon to be highlighted in the sermon. (Cf. the comments on the sign quality of miracle in the exegesis of today's Gospel.) In truth, what lies behind the miracle is what the author is saying about God and our relation to him as a result of his revelation. This fact should be uppermost in the preacher's mind as he deals with passages such as these.

First Lesson. This lesson presents the preacher with at least three possible lines of sermon development. 1. The towering figure of *Elijah* gives ample material for an effective biblical sermon based on his life and work. Through this brief incident one could move into other references which could flesh out this most important prophet. He was a mighty force in the early Hebrew tradition and his memory was carried into the NT. Even Jesus was thought by some to be Elijah returned (Matt. 16:14; Luke 9:8). John was also so considered (John 1:21). Such a sermon would include not only his miraculous feats, but certainly his struggle against the worshipers of Baal and especially his contesting with kings on behalf of God. The latter two facets alone are pregnant with possibilities when we consider both the modern-day equivalents of Baal worship on the one hand and civic or national religion on the other.

2. A subsidiary but important theme in these verses concerns the relationship between *affliction* and *sin*. The woman attributes the death of her son to the presence of Elijah. Many believed that the presence of the man of God brought to light a person's former sins—hidden or otherwise—and certainly the woman considered Elijah in that light. Even Elijah assumed the death of the boy to be God's act. This problem of connecting sin and tragedy is a perennial one and many people in our own day relate misfortune to the presence of sin. Though other

places in Scripture might present an even better basis for a sermon on this theme, certainly the opportunity for treatment of this important topic is here.

3. The obvious theme presented is the general one of the role of the *prophet.* Though similar to number one above, the stress would not be on the life of Elijah as much as it would be on his work as a prophet (cf. exegesis of today's Gospel). It could lead to developing the nature of prophecy in the Hebrew-Christian tradition; the relation of priest to prophet; the difference between prophecy and soothsaying; and the perils and promises of relating the prophetic to the church's ministry today.

Second Lesson. This lesson picks up where last Sunday's Second Lesson left off. Paul is attempting to vindicate his apostleship. In so doing he recounts in his own words how the revelation which occurred on the Damascus road (Acts 9) turned him from a pious persecutor of the Christians into a preacher of the faith. These autobiographical words, along with the distinctive note of his being chosen and predestined to be a preacher of the gospel, fit in with the theme of the three lessons and afford sermonic treatment either in connection with the other two passages or on their own merits.

As in the case of Elijah, Paul's own life could be the basis of a sermon. This pericope could simply be the prism through which we would look at not only his autobiographical recounting of his apostolic ministry in his epistles but also the stories of his missionary work in Acts. Such a portrait of St. Paul would get a receptive hearing from modern persons who like others in the history of the Christian church have had a "Damascus road" experience of Jesus Christ. Further, the fact that Paul had not seen Jesus in the flesh and did not consider himself one of the inner circle of apostles, makes it easy for us to relate to him. Paul felt his experience was as authentic as that of the apostles who were with Jesus; therefore, we too who live by faith rather than sight have St. Paul not only as a teacher but as a brother in spirit.

Gospel. Whatever else we might believe about the incarnation and Jesus' consciousness of messiahship, it is clear in the Gospel lesson that Jesus is in the prophetic tradition. There are two obvious reasons for this judgment in relating the Luke passage to the others: 1. After he had healed the widow's son, the people proclaimed him a prophet. In last Sunday's pericope and immediately preceding this incident, Jesus had healed the centurion's son without receiving such an accolade. 2. There are obvious parallels between this passage and the one in 1

Kings (cf. exegesis). The ability to perform mighty deeds in the name of God was in the prophetic tradition and not alone reserved for the Divine One.

At the same time, there is a new note in this passage and it is not surprising to the Christian. In v. 13, Jesus is addressed as *Lord* for the first time. (See notes in JB, e.g.: "For the first time in the Gospel narrative, Jesus is given the title hitherto reserved for Yahweh himself.") Comparing this pericope with the one which goes before and with the subsequent verses concerning Jesus' answer to the disciples of John, it is possible for the preacher to see the developing lordship of Christ. He is undoubtedly within the prophetic tradition in Luke's mind, but he is also something more (see v. 26). Jesus as a prophet and as "something more" leads the minister into the heart of christological preaching. Such a theme is a natural focal point of the three lessons for this day.

The NAB translation presents an interesting homiletical footnote which could set off the preacher's imagination. V. 24 reads, "and they gave glory to God on my account." While the other versions have the same meaning, the freshness of these words is arresting. To ask the simple question, "Does my life as a Christian cause others to give glory to God?" can lead to a penetrating examination of the life of the Christian.

The Fourth Sunday after Pentecost

Lutheran	*Roman Catholic*	*Episcopal*	*Presbyterian and UCC*
2 Sam. 12:1–10, 13	2 Sam. 12:7–10, 13	2 Sam. 12:7–10, 13	2 Sam. 12:1–7a
Gal. 2:11–21	Gal. 2:16, 19–21	Gal. 2:11–21	Gal. 2:15–21
Luke 7:36–8:3	Luke 7:36–50	Luke 7:36–50	Luke 7:36–50

EXEGESIS

First Lesson: 2 Sam. 12:1–10, 13. This lesson is from the "Succession Document" or court history of David (2 Samuel 9–20; 1 Kings 1–2), one of the most vivid narratives of the OT. The immediate context is the conclusion to the story of David's adultery with Bathsheba and his contrived murder of Uriah.

The lesson is divided into the confrontation between prophet and king (cf. 1 Sam. 15:17–24, Saul and Samuel; 1 Kings 18 ff., Ahab and Elijah) in the form of a parable spoken by Nathan. The form and function of a parable are superbly illustrated here. A parable is basically a comparison where the surface meaning conceals a deeper meaning. To understand the parable the hearer must enter the world of the parable and this entrance carries the risk of self-revelation (cf. today's Gospel, Luke 7:40–44, where the one addressed becomes the one confronted). Nathan's parable might be called a parable on "the arrogance of power" since the point is the caprice and injustice of the rich man. It is this injustice which precipitates David's reaction (vv. 5–6) since, as king, he is anointed to uphold justice in the land (2 Sam. 8:15).

In vv. 7 ff. Nathan applies the parable to David and delivers an oracle of the Lord which shows that the real malice of David's sin is not so much murder and adultery as his lack of fidelity to his anointed role. The punishment will be in kind. The violence which David showed in his act will be visited on his house (i.e., family), as the subsequent stories of Ammon (13:1–38) and Absalom (15:1–37) illustrate. The repentance of David is found in the simple confession of v. 13, "I have sinned against the Lord." In the OT this acknowledgement or self-appropriation of the sinful act is a prelude to receiving the Lord's ready forgiveness (Jer. 2:35, "Behold I will bring you to judgment for saying: 'I have not sinned'"; cf. Pss. 41:4; 51:4; Job 33:26–28). Nathan then pronounces the forgiveness of David. According to the exact law of retribution he should die, but he will not for the Lord has "put away" his sin. The verb "put away" literally means "has caused to pass over" and is a rare usage here. It carries the idea that, though the Lord will not exact the full penalty for David's sin, the effect of the evil must be played out.

Second Lesson: Gal. 2:11–21. The Second Lesson is divided into two sections: vv. 11–14, the account of Cephas's inconsistency and backsliding from the Jerusalem agreement and Paul's answer (vv. 15–21) which forms a résumé of his gospel, directed now more to the situation in Galatia, than to Cephas. The disagreement with Cephas is a necessary prelude to vv. 15–21 for it shows that the issue was "our freedom which we have in Christ Jesus" (2:4). More importantly, it also shows that Paul writes in the context of a Christian dispute. He is not writing a theoretical apology to Jews on law and gospel, but is attempting to show how the gospel would be perverted (1:7) if Jewish Christians who believe in Christ were to return to the law as a source of justification or if Gentile converts were forced (2:14, "you compel") to observe the works of the law (2:16).

The argument in 2:15–21 is complex. The beginning (vv. 15–16) might be paraphrased as: If we who were Jews are justified (i.e., made or declared upright) by faith and not by doing what the law commands (since even we do not accept the law in its totality), why should Gentiles who were never under the law be compelled to observe it? The following verse (17) is a standard Pauline device, a dialogue with an imaginary objector (cf. Rom. 2:1 ff.; 6:1 ff.). The force of the implied objection is that, since the law is from God, not to observe it is sinful, and then Christ would be an agent of sin. This objection is answered not in v. 18 but in v. 19 and the first half of v. 20: "I through the law died to the law that I might live to God. I have been crucified with Christ." In turn this verse is best understood in light of 2:21 and 3:13, "Christ redeemed us from the curse of the law, having become a curse." Just as Christ through or because of the law died to the law, so the Christian "crucified" with Christ is dead to the law (cf. Rom. 6:11; 7:4; 2 Cor. 5:15). Paul attributes to the law a mentality which was responsible for the death of Christ, so that for the Christian there is no option of returning to the law.

In vv. 20*b*–21 Paul spells out the consequences of justification by faith. The life of the Christian is life "with Christ" (or as Paul states one hundred sixty-four times, "in Christ"). The quality of the life Christ lived and his self-giving even to death are normative. This life is, however, still in the flesh (v. 20), i.e., limited by the sinful condition of man. Paul shuns any mystic escapism, such as he will later encounter in Corinth. Finally this life is lived *in faith* which is a deep personal realization that the Son of God *loved me* and *gave himself for me* (v. 20). Paul's gospel is not an "answer" to the opponents at Galatia. It is an invitation to respond to the true meaning of faith.

Gospel: Luke 7:36–50. The tradition behind this narrative is complex since variations of it are found in Mark 14:3–9; Matt. 26:6–13; and John 12:1–8. Since interpretation is often colored by the variations, certain clarifications must be made. In Luke the woman is unnamed and, though a sinner, her sin is unspecified—she could be either a prostitute or married to a man with a sinful occupation, e.g., a tax collector. In Luke 7:36 the host is Simon the Pharisee; in Mark and Matthew, Simon the leper, and in John the incident takes place in the house of Martha and Mary. In Luke the incident takes place in Galilee, during the early stages of the ministry; elsewhere near Jerusalem, as a prelude to the passion. In Luke and John the woman anoints the feet of Jesus; in Mark and Matthew, his head. Also, caution should be observed against identifying the woman of Luke with either "Mary called Magdalene" (8:2) or Mary, the sister of Martha (10:39, 42).

The narrative begins with the familiar Lucan scene of Jesus sharing table fellowship (5:29; 7:36; 10:38; 11:37; 14:1; 19:5). The drama comes when Jesus accepts the woman and the honor she pays him. The

disapproval of the Pharisee is typical of the Pharisees' attitude toward
Jesus' table fellowship with the outcasts of his time (5:30; 7:34; 15:2),
and the parable (vv. 41–42) is an answer to him. The point of the parable is in Simon's grudging admission ("I suppose") that the forgiven one
loves more. Jesus then turns to the Pharisee and indicts him in rhythmic
contrast between his lack of concern and the woman's care (vv. 44–46).
He then proclaims the forgiveness of the woman "for she loved much."
It has been disputed whether this phrase should be interpreted either
as "she was forgiven because she loved" or "she loved because she was
forgiven." The citation of the meaning of the parable "he who is forgiven
little, loves little" shows that the second interpretation of "for she loved
much" is the proper one. The love of the woman is a response to forgiving
love; this brought her to Jesus; for this Jesus praised her. The final verse
of the narrative (v. 50) "your faith has saved you" repeats a phrase
usually associated with the healing miracles (cf. Pentecost 2: exegesis of
the Gospel). The forgiveness of sins is no less a healing than physical
healing. It too begins in faith. This narrative is a beautiful illustration
of Luke's *Gospel of Mercy*, and is itself a parable of the loving forgiveness of God which creates in a person the ability to accept God's love.

HOMILETICAL INTERPRETATION

One way to look at the lessons for this Sunday is to see *conflict* within
the household of faith: David and Nathan; Paul and Peter (Cephas);
Jesus and the Pharisees. Or, the relationship between *law* and *gospel*. Or,
the forgiveness of sins. David broke the moral law, but repented and was
forgiven; Paul reiterated justification by faith rather than the Mosaic
code in his continuing struggle with the Judaizers; Jesus' relationship
with the sinners represented again his contention of love and forgiveness
instead of the rigid posture of the Pharisees.

First Lesson. The story of Nathan and David is one of the most
familiar stories in the Bible and familiarity—if not breeding contempt—
often results in staleness. However, this ancient confrontation between a
prophet and his king has contemporaneity on at least two levels. 1. We
often need reminding that in the Hebrew-Christian tradition the prophetic role has always brought God's spokesmen into conflict with the rulers
of state. In times when the periodic cry of "keep the pulpit out of
politics" is heard, it is necessary to remind ourselves of the prophetic
responsibility each minister carries. 2. The pattern of judgment in this
passage is worth observing. David judges himself. Long before the advent
of nondirective counseling, Nathan told an oblique parable which en-
meshed David in its fabric so that when he judged the rich man in the

story he was really pronouncing his own guilt. David simply needed to observe the parallel. Much of our condemnation of sin and sinners has been on the level of scolding, judgmental pronouncements, and tiresome moral tirades which often produce defensiveness rather than repentance. David saw his own sin, made his own judgment, and so his confession came from inner-motivated repentance.

Another interesting motif in this pericope is the perennially over-looked fact that David's sin is really against the Lord. After the clarity of his judgment, the king rightly states in v. 13, "I have sinned against the Lord." So much of the time we believe the moral codes are always man-made and easily bent by our peccadillos, but as this story reminds us, sin against other persons is really against God for he is the author of our morality and justice. "It is God who sets the moral standard, not man" (notes, RSV, Oxford edition).

Finally, the poignant theme of repentance and forgiveness is seen here in a most dramatic way. We Christians need to be reminded that one does not need to wait for the NT in order to see love and forgiveness. David confessed his sin and was forgiven. Of course, in early biblical history we do see a morality of retaliation and even here David's son died, but it is equally true that repentance elicits forgiveness as it does in this ancient story.

Second Lesson. Paul here continues his struggle with the Judaizers over law and gospel. This time the quarrel is with Peter who seemingly has accepted the Gentile Christians by eating with them and then with-draws from that fellowship when the Jerusalem party rebukes him. It is this issue which provokes Paul's wrath. This particular tension between Jewish and Gentile Christians has been with us before in the lessons, so much of what has been said would apply here. One other approach that is worth exploring is the nature of conflict within the church. At one time many believed that Christians never quarreled, never lost their tempers, nor otherwise engaged in combative behavior. Thus, all political, social, and personal differences were left outside the church and after crossing the threshold we were all to be amiable Christlike people. Certainly in the last few years we have seen Christian people confronting one another over the issues of war, race, and social justice. The preacher's task may be to help Christians handle their conflicts creatively—placing those contentions under the judgment of God—rather than attempting to stifle them. These verses remind us that this problem is not a new one and the early church was filled with confrontation—Christian style.

The other powerful idea in these verses is the restatement of what is Paul's basic teaching. It is, of course, justification by faith and we have seen that theme before in these Pentecost lessons. There are two things, though, that are especially striking in this particular pericope. 1. Paul tackles the charge often made—then and now—that if we are saved by Christ from sin and not through our own works by law observance, then Christ must be encouraging sin. Or, to put it another way, if we are excused from the law are we free to do as we please? Paul's answers to that are curt and to the point as reflected in the various translations. "No, never!" "Certainly not!" "Absurd." "Unthinkable!" 2. What Paul substitutes for the law is not antinomianism (i.e., since man is saved by grace and not works then he is free from all moral effort), but a new creation. Then, in one of the most powerful texts in the Bible he tells what this new man in Christ is like: "I have been crucified with Christ, and the life I live now is not my own; Christ is living in me. I still live my human life, but it is a life of faith in the Son of God, who loved me and gave himself for me" (NAB). Thus, the Christian cannot return to the old ways for "The living acts of a Christian become somehow the acts of Christ" (notes in JB).

Gospel. The incident recorded in Luke has parallels in the other Gospels and represents Jesus' continuing disagreement with the Pharisees over the relationship of the sinners to the righteous. There are at least four interesting approaches to this body of scriptural material. 1. In relation to Simon, Jesus is pointing out that he does not know the meaning of forgiveness. He was concerned about the woman being a sinner; Jesus was interested in her love and forgave her of her sins. Simon loved little and forgave little. Simon's superiority kept him from seeing his own sinfulness even though it may have been less than the woman's. 2. Focusing on the woman, Jesus was impressed by the commitment of the uncommitted—as he always was. Her anointing—at the very least an act of great respect—evoked great love and even though she had sinned greatly she loved greatly, thus receiving great forgiveness. 3. It is extremely interesting to note how Jesus got into trouble with the righteous. He did not receive their wrath because he healed the sick; he incurred antagonisms because he not only consorted with sinners, but more importantly, he forgave sins. To the Pharisees this must have seemed like idolatry; to Luke it was surely acknowledgement of his sonship. 4. The Bible records the importance of women in the early church (cf. Pentecost 3: exegesis of the Gospel). The beginning of the eighth chapter records a brief travelogue which points up the place of women in Jesus' ministry. The NAB notes point out that the writer evidently has in mind the contributions of women to the early Christian community. So he should and so should we.

The Fifth Sunday after Pentecost

Lutheran	Roman Catholic	Episcopal	Presbyterian and UCC
Zech. 12:7–10	Zech. 12:10–11	Zech. 12:9–11	Zech. 12:7–10
Gal. 3:26–29	Gal. 3:26–29	Gal. 3:23–29	Gal. 3:23–29
Luke 9:18–24	Luke 9:18–24	Luke 9:18–24	Luke 9:18–24

EXEGESIS

First Lesson: Zech. 12:7–10. The latter chapters of Zechariah (9–14) are recognized as additions to the work of the historical Zechariah (c. 520 B.C.). The emergence of apocalyptic motifs (persecution, suffering, and the struggles of the last days, 12:3 ff.; 14; the hope of victory and the universal reign of the Lord, 14:9), the lack of clear historical references, in contrast to Zechariah 1–8, and the great number of allusions to the classical prophets suggest a date in the Greek period (c. 300–200 B.C.). This latter part of Zechariah is cited or alluded to at least thirty-nine times in the NT and provides a storehouse of texts which were used in telling the story of the passion of Jesus—9:9, "your king is coming" (Matt. 21:5; John 12:15); 9:11, "the blood of my covenant" (Mark 14:24, et par.; 1 Cor. 11:25; Heb. 13:20); 13:7–9, "strike the shepherd and the sheep will be scattered" (Mark 14:27, 50 et par.; John 16:32); "thirty shekels of silver" (Matt. 26:15; 27:9); 12:10, "when they look on him whom they have pierced" (John 19:37; Rev. 1:7). The theme of these chapters, that the victory will come only after suffering, provided the NT writers with an understanding of the horror of the passion as a prelude to the victory of the resurrection.

The section 12:7–10 is the promise of victory to the Davidic house (vv. 7–9) and the beginning of the great lament (vv. 10–11). In v. 10 the Lord will pour out his spirit (cf. Isa. 44:3; Ezek. 39:29; Joel 2:28), a spirit of "compassion and supplication." "Compassion" is not the best translation of the Hebrew; "spirit of grace" (NAB) is more accurate. In v. 10 the lament of the people begins when they "look on him whom they have pierced." The Hebrew is obscure here and reads literally: "on me whom they have pierced." Interpreters reject any notion that the Lord has been pierced and propose an alternate translation: "They shall look on me concerning the one they pierced." Despite this difficulty the major motif remains that the repentance which precedes the glorious end is evoked by turning to the vicarious suffering of an individual, whether he be a martyred prophet, or some symbolic figure like the servant in Isa. 52:13–53:12.

Second Lesson: Gal. 3:26–29. The Second Lesson is from Paul's
scriptural proof that faith, not the law, saves man (3:1–31). Paul has just
compared the law to a custodian charged with watching over a minor
child. The coming of Christ (3:24–25), "the end of the law" (Rom.
10:4), brought freedom from such a custodian. "For in Christ Jesus you
are all sons of God through faith" (v. 26): In the OT, "son of God" is
used of kings, specially anointed individuals, and the whole people of
Israel. Paul thus conveys not only the adoptive sonship of the Christian
(Gal. 4:4–6; Rom. 8:15–17) but also his status in the new Israel of God
(Gal. 6:16). "Baptized into Christ" (v. 27): The preposition "into"
means "in union with" (cf. Rom. 6:3; 1 Cor. 1:13; 10:2; 12:13). For
Paul, baptism is not only a consequence of faith but a public manifestation of adherence to Christ. "Put on Christ" (v. 27): The image is one
of "investiture" with a new status and new dignity (cf. Col. 3:10; Eph.
4:24, "put on the new man").

"There is neither Jew nor Greek. . . ." (v. 28; cf. Rom. 10:12): Faith,
leading to baptism, creates a new community, knit together by a bond
which surmounts differences of race, social status, and sex. This verse
and Rom. 10:12 must always be considered in counterbalance to Paul's
culturally conditioned attitude toward slavery (Philemon) and women
(1 Cor. 7; 11:2–16), and to his polemical attitudes toward the Jewish
law. Paul concludes this section, returning to the figure of Abraham (3:7,
"it is men of faith who are the sons of Abraham") whereby he sees a
unity in God's saving plan from Abraham to Christ, and at the same time
prepares the way for the discussion of the adoptive sonship of the Christian which is the inheritance of Abraham ("heirs according to promise,"
v. 29).

Gospel: Luke 9:18–24. This section represents the confession of
Peter, the first of three passion predictions, and sayings on discipleship,
which are found in all the Synoptics (1. Luke 9:19–27; Matt. 16:13–28;
Mark 8:27–38; 2. Luke 9:43*b*–45; Matt. 17:22–23; Mark 9:30–32; 3.
Luke 18:31–34; Matt. 20:17–19; Mark 10:32–34). In Mark and Matthew
these three predictions form a careful unity and come at the turning
point in their Gospels when Jesus leaves Galilee and begins his way to
Jerusalem from Caesarea Philippi. Luke breaks this unity and places the
first two predictions in the context of Jesus' Galilean ministry. The rear-
rangement of his sources by Luke suggests that he sees the foreshadow-
ing of suffering as an integral part of the whole ministry of Jesus.

"Now it happened that as he was praying" (v. 18): Only Luke places
the first prediction in the context of Jesus praying, in harmony with the
explicit Lucan view that Jesus is at prayer before important events (3:21,

baptism; 6:12, the choice of the twelve; 9:18, before the transfiguration; 11:1, before the Lord's Prayer; 22:41, at Gethsemane). The question and answer of vv. 18*b*–20 contrast the popular view that Jesus is either John or Elijah returned or one of the prophets with the answer of Peter that Jesus is "the Christ [anointed] of God." This answer has two facets: (a) Jesus is not a forerunner of the Messiah (Christ); (b) he is the anointed "of God." By the addition "of God" to his Marcan source Luke stresses that Jesus is more than the Messiah in whom the OT promises are fulfilled; he is *the one* in whom and through whom God's saving history is now manifest. In v. 22 the prediction of suffering immediately follows the confession stressing that confession involves a willingness to "come after" Jesus on the way of the cross. In using "Son of man" here Luke follows the tradition of the church which used the figure of the triumphant Son of man from Dan. 7:13 ff. to link together the future triumphant coming of Christ (e.g. Mark 13:26; 14:62 *et par.*), the earthly ministry of Jesus (Mark 2:1–12 *et par.*), and the suffering of Jesus.

In the sayings on discipleship (vv. 23–24) which join together the way of Jesus and the way of the disciple, Luke has the important addition "take up his cross *daily*." Similar Lucan additions occur in the Lord's Prayer: "give us *each day* our daily bread," and in the saying on forgiveness: "if he sins against you seven times *in the day*" (17:3–4). These additions suggest a shift in Luke's eschatology where he sees Jesus' words addressed not simply to the impending crisis of Jesus' death, but to a church faced with an open future where suffering, loss of life, and finding it in the following of Jesus become a daily challenge.

HOMILETICAL INTERPRETATION

Whatever other unity may be found in the three lessons for today, it is clear that Christology is raised as a preeminent theme. The preacher should always be wary of reading christological inferences into OT passages, but in today's lesson it is clear that the pierced one referred to resembles the suffering servant concept in Isaiah. In addition, John refers to this very passage when describing the crucifixion of Jesus. In Galatians, Paul affirms the unity brought about through Jesus Christ and in Luke the affirmation is made that Jesus is the Christ. In both NT passages, incidentally, Jesus is connected in one way or another with the OT.

First Lesson. The pericope from Zechariah suggests a large area for the preacher's attention under the category of the messianic age. In this lesson attention is drawn to the restoration of Jerusalem, the age to come, and the introduction of the theme of the suffering servant. As indicated above, when this lesson is seen from the perspective of the evangelist John, then it is clear that the OT prophet gives a background and setting for the figure of Jesus Christ who is unveiled in the New. (Among other passages, the preacher will want to study Isa. 52:13–53:12 and John 19:37 referred to above.)

Though the messianic motif may be the major one in the First Lesson, there are other notable ideas, though possibly less important than the one indicated. For one thing, God's protection of his people is an ever-present motif in biblical history. Also, the restoration of Jerusalem with all that city means in Israelite history—both literally and figuratively—has importance as a theme right down to the present day. (Cf. The Day of Pentecost and Pentecost 7: exegesis of the Second Lesson.)

Second Lesson. Paul states again in summary form his understanding of the gospel. As is often the case, he can put in capsule-like brevity the essence of the good news brought about by Jesus Christ. These three verses are no exception. Though the preacher should never be limited slavishly to the structure provided by a pericope, it is clear that this passage unfolds both exegetically and homiletically along the following lines: 1. Christ has made us all sons through faith, 2. in baptism we have put on Christ as a garment, 3. Christ has brought unity, and 4. we are heirs of Abraham, the man of faith. Whether one thinks of this structure as one specific sermon or as several, the outline permits the preacher to develop his thinking along a clear pattern of development.

1. *All sons through faith:* Paul here recapitulates the doctrine of justification by faith. He has just finished saying that the law was like a teacher which prepared us for Christ's coming. But now through faith in Christ we are no longer under a guardian; instead we are sons of God. The whole concept of "sons of God" is arresting as one makes the distinction between natural man and son. Familial analogies can be helpful here if not carried too far.

2. *Baptized into union with Christ:* Paul makes a powerful statement as to the importance of baptism. For one thing, he does not contrast faith and baptism (cf. Rom. 6:4 ff.). We are tempted to forget the importance of baptism as a means of grace—whatever the mode. One of the most common examples is the talk of having an experience of Christ by church people who are obviously baptized. This is not to denigrate the experiences of faith that come to people whether baptized or not. At the same time, there is a danger of supposing that the baptism of the church is somehow invalid until given an emotional experience. An experience may certify for a Christian a feeling of faith, but baptism itself is a means of grace and brings us into union with Jesus Christ.

3. *All are one in Christ*: If there is any need to emphasize our common denominator with all peoples, here is one of the key biblical texts. There are simply no distinctions among men: race, sex, status—all melt away in union with Christ. If we do permit these distinctions to arise, then we have broken the union with Jesus Christ.

4. *Heirs of Abraham*: The motif of sons, adoption, and heirs is carried out by Paul as he relates the Christian to Abraham. There are two obvious connections worth noting. For one thing, he links the Christian to God's continuing revelation which began in the OT with covenant relationships such as Abraham's. Second, there is spiritual kinship with Abraham as he is typical of all men of faith (cf. Hebrews 11). Being his offspring means that the Christian is part of the covenant promise made by God to Abraham and fulfilled in the coming of Christ.

Gospel. The acme of the christological theme is found in the Gospel where Jesus himself asks the disciples who they think he is. Their answer and Peter's confession is the heart of the Christian faith and focuses on the statement that has been the cornerstone of the Christian church. This great theological theme of the person and work of Christ will provide as much or more than one sermon can possibly include. In addition, though, there are two other thrusts which may have a great deal of merit. One, the relationship of Jesus to Elijah, John the Baptist, and the other prophets, can be a theme all by itself. While certainly involved in the person of Christ, the specific thought here would be Jesus in comparison with the other prophetic figures in Hebrew history, the line of continuity in which he falls, and the culmination of the messianic hopes. Part of this is the import of that recognition to the disciples.

The second thrust, Peter's confession itself, goes beyond the simple recognition that his Master had become his Lord. In some ways the question is more important than the answer. For the question goes beyond the general one of "Who do people say that I am?" to the existential one of "Who do *you* think that I am?" Or, even more pointedly, "But you, who do you say I am?" (JB). The difference between the question of who do people *say* Jesus is and who do *you* think he is demonstrates the difference between knowledge *about* Christ and faith *in* him. Many Christians have a general faith in or belief about Jesus Christ, but faith takes on a different meaning entirely when the question is addressed to each person directly. Such a question as Jesus asked takes the Christian out of the ranks of the spectator and places him in the arena.

The other half of the pericope focuses on discipleship and of course leads naturally from the confession. If one believes that Jesus is the Christ, then it is inevitable that something follows that affirmation. What follows is discipleship. Without the confession there would be no need for discipleship, but having made the confession there are conditions which follow. Though these conditions are repeated throughout the Gospel and are expanded in different parallels, there are two aspects held up in this pericope. First, bearing one's cross daily. The preacher's most difficult job is to make "cross bearing" a real act of discipleship rather than a euphemism for simply being a church-goer. The challenge is to think of ways that being a Christian is or should be a risk. Second, the paradox of losing one's life in order to save it goes against so much of what we normally believe that most Christians are perhaps embarrassed by such a saying. Standing on end some of our most precious standards is the most challenging work of the pulpit. Dramatizing this particular one can go a long way in making discipleship come alive in the Christian church today.

The Sixth Sunday after Pentecost

Lutheran	*Roman Catholic*	*Episcopal*	*Presbyterian and UCC*
1 Kings 19:14-21	1 Kings 19:16b, 19-21	1 Kings 19:15-16, 19-21	1 Kings 19:15-21
Gal. 5:1, 13-25	Gal. 4:31b-5:1, 13-18	Gal. 4:31-5:1, 13-18	Gal. 5:1, 13-18
Luke 9:51-62	Luke 9:51-62	Luke 9:51-62	Luke 9:51-62

EXEGESIS

First Lesson: 1 Kings 19:14–21. The lesson is from the larger context which describes Elijah's flight (19:3), the comforting by an angel and his forty day sojourn in the wilderness (19:3-8—the wilderness in the OT is the place of trial and of revelation), the revelation to Elijah (19:9-13), his mission (14-17), and the call of Elisha (19-21).

In 19:11-13 the presence of the Lord is described in language much like the revelation to Moses at Sinai (Exod. 19:16 ff.). The initial words of Elijah in v. 14 are a response to the Lord's question: "What are you doing here, Elijah?" The question is also a veiled rebuke of Elijah's hesitancy before the prophetic challenge. Elijah's excuse that he is jealous for the Lord is met by the Lord's imperative: "Go, return" (19:15). The prophet is a prophet when he is doing or proclaiming the word of the Lord. Elijah is given a threefold commission: to anoint Hazael (c. 841-798 B.C.) as king of Syria, to anoint Jehu (842-815 B.C.) as king of Israel, and to anoint Elisha as his successor (the command to anoint Elisha is unique in prophetic literature). Though these "anointings" are not done by Elijah, the command of the Lord indicates his sovereign power over history. All power, royal or prophetic, comes from him. "I will leave seven thousand" (v. 18): This is an anticipation of the idea of the "remnant" which becomes important in the classical prophets (Amos 3:12; 5:3; 9:12 ff.; Isa. 4:2; 7:3 ff.; 10:20–22; 11:10–16; 28:5; 37:4), in the postexilic literature (Isa. 65:8–10; Hag. 1:12–14; 2:2; Zech. 8:6 ff.; Ezra 9:8, 14–15; Neh. 1:2–3), and in the NT (Rom. 9–11).

The "call" of Elisha (i.e. "God is salvation") begins with the symbolic action of Elijah clothing him in the distinctive prophetic garb, the hair skin coat (mantle); cf. 2 Kings 1:8; Zech. 13:4; Matt. 3:4. Since the mantle was in intimate contact with the man of God, it was thought to be imbued with his power (2 Kings 2:14, cf. Mark 5:28; Matt. 9:21; Luke 8:44, the woman who touches Jesus' garment). The following verse contains Elisha's request "to kiss my father and my mother" (cf. Luke 9:61) and Elijah's enigmatic response: "Go back again; for what have I done to you?" A paraphrase of the Hebrew text as either "Go ahead, for have I done anything to stop you?" or "Go, but remember what I have told you" expresses the uncompromising nature of the prophetic call. The sacrifice of the oxen in v. 21 symbolizes Elisha's break with his old manner of life, celebrated in a common meal before he embarks ("he arose and went") on a new task.

Second Lesson: Gal. 5:1, 13–25. "For freedom Christ has set us free" (5:1): Paul begins the hortatory part of the letter with a succinct statement of one of the major themes of the letter. Freedom is at the same time a present gift to the Christian ("has set us free," perfect tense), and the goal of Christian life ("for freedom," dative of purpose). Christian freedom is liberation from sin, from the law, and from death. In the remaining verses (13–26) Paul simultaneously cautions against the misuse of freedom (vv. 13, 16–21) and portrays the quality of life in true freedom (vv. 13*b*, 14, 22–26). The opposition between flesh and spirit in these verses is not between the physical and spiritual side of man, but between man as a whole living according to the flesh, i.e., standing in opposition to God's plan, or according to the spirit, i.e., living open to God's free gift.

"Be servants of one another. For the whole law is fulfilled in one word" (cf. Lev. 19:18; Matt. 5:43–44; 19:19; 22:39; Mark 12:31; Luke 10:27; Rom. 13:9): The basis of a Christian ethic of freedom is a life of servanthood (cf. Phil. 2:3–11; Rom. 15:1–7; 2 Cor. 5:14–15; 8:7–9) where unity and harmony replace dominion (v. 15). In 5:17 Paul envisions the life of

Christian freedom as a struggle (Rom. 7:15–23) and characterizes life in
slavery to the flesh by a traditional list of vices (Rom. 1:29–31; 1 Cor. 6:
9 ff.; Col. 3:5–7; Eph. 4:31; 5:3 ff.). ". . . shall not inherit the Kingdom
of God": The kingdom is for Paul both a present reality, manifest in
God's action through Christ, and a future hope (cf. 1 Thess. 2:12; 2
Thess. 1:5). Note that Paul contrasts the *works* of the flesh with the *fruit*
of the Spirit; he never speaks of the *works* of the Spirit. The good actions
of the Christian grow freely and spontaneously out of his life in Christ. In
v. 25 Paul again joins the Christian proclamation to a Christian ethic.
Paul is not talking only about a psychological awareness of life in the
Spirit, but a radical orientation which will change a man's life. In this
whole section Paul recognizes a tension between the gift given and the
fullness of the gift when total freedom is achieved. Christian discipleship
is always lived between promise and fulfillment.

Gospel: Luke 9:51–62. The Gospel is from the beginning of the
second major section of Luke, the "travel narrative" (9:51–19:28), recounting Jesus' journey to Jerusalem. In this section Luke departs from his
Marcan source and the material is either from Q or from his own
source. Just as the first major section of the Gospel begins with a rejection (4:14–30), so too does this section (9:53).

V. 51 serves as introduction to this section. "When the days drew
near": The literal translation "and it came to pass when the days were
fulfilled" captures better the solemn beginning which the Hebraizing style
connotes and the sense of a new stage in saving history (cf. Acts 2:1).
"To be received up": Literally, for his taking up or ascension. This is the
same term used of Elijah's translation (2 Kings 2:9–11) and of the ascension of Jesus (Acts 1:2, 11, 22). "He set his face": This is an OT usage
(Isa. 50:7; Ezek. 6:2; 13:17; 14:8) which describes firmness of purpose
in the face of hostility and rejection. "To Jerusalem": (For the role of
Jerusalem in Luke, cf. The Day of Pentecost: exegesis of Second Lesson.)
The added emphasis here is on Jerusalem as the locale of a prophet's
death (Luke 13:31–34) and on the fact that Jesus on his *way up* to Jerusalem will teach the community what it must be as it moves *outward
from* Jerusalem.

V. 53 tells of the rejection of Jesus by the Samaritans. Hostility between the Jews and the Samaritans is well attested in the NT (cf. John
4:9; 8:48). The reaction of the disciples (v. 54) mirrors such hostility and
at the same time continues the Elijah motif (cf. 2 Kings 1:10, "If I am
a man of God, let fire come down from heaven and consume you."").
Jesus rejects such a vindication of his mission and "they went on to
another village," an illustration of Luke 9:5.

The nature of discipleship is the subject of vv. 57–62. The three sayings on following Jesus occur "on the way." The way is not only the way or journey to Jerusalem, but also the "way" of following Jesus (cf. Acts 9:2; the early Christians are called "those belonging to the way"). The conditions of discipleship are set out in three parable-like sayings. The first two are paralleled in Matt. 8:19–22 and the third is a Lucan addition. In response to the first, Jesus promises only a pilgrim existence, which Jesus' own rejections embody. The second incident is not a request, but an invitation ("follow me"). In view of traditional Jewish filial piety (cf. Gen. 49:28–50:3; Tob. 4:3; 6:14), the words of Jesus (v. 60) appear especially harsh. A common interpretation is to spiritualize the saying of Jesus: "let the spiritually dead (i.e. those who don't follow) bury the physically dead." It seems better, however, to see the words as a symbolic proclamation of the depth and intensity of the call "to proclaim the kingdom." The third request (v. 61) is suggested by the call of Elisha and emphasizes the prophetic nature of Christian discipleship. The three sayings on discipleship express the radical nature of Jesus' preaching of the kingdom of God. Such a radical call to man demands an equally radical freedom on the part of man to respond (cf. the Second Lesson).

HOMILETICAL INTERPRETATION

The preacher seeking an immediately apparent unifying theme in these pericopes may be disappointed. As has been pointed out, he does not need to do so and can proceed with the individual lessons. On the other hand, one way to address these scripture passages is under the heading, "The Call to Commitment." In the passage from Kings, the call involves both Elijah's response to God and Elisha's response to Elijah's call to share the prophetic mission. The Gospel seems to parallel the OT, for the pericope relates Jesus' own commitment in relation to his going to Jerusalem and it tells of the demands of discipleship on his followers. The Galatians passage may not seem to fit the pattern as well as the other two, but the commitment here is to freedom rather than law and the resultant responsibility of loving one's neighbor as oneself—an obligation of discipleship.

First Lesson. In the First Lesson for the Third Sunday after Pentecost we have already been introduced to the figure of Elijah. Much of the material given there is appropriate for the present Sunday. In addition, other themes present themselves uniquely in this passage. For one, the call of the prophet is especially strong in this lesson. The minister may be tempted to see the passage in terms of the preacher as prophet; this is a legitimate interpretation. The role of the preacher-prophet in the Christian church needs holding up again and again so the prophetic passages are not only for the ears of ministers. Also, what is said about prophets is easily applicable to all people of God, for the twin categories of call and response are at the heart of the religious life.

First of all, we see the call of the prophet. Preceding this section of verses is the familiar recounting of the earthquake, wind, and fire—all of which were the places where man might be expected to encounter God as in Exodus 19, for example. Here, though, God appeared in a still, small voice or "the sound of a gentle breeze" (JB). It is important to point out that the soft encounter does not mean that God's demands are gentle; it simply suggests that God was intimate with his prophets and he is a Spirit (see notes on passage in JB).

The second thing to note is the peril of the prophet: in this case, his loneliness highlighted in v. 14. He is brokenhearted because the people have been unfaithful and he is alone. The loneliness of the man of God is mirrored in all of the church's history and modern examples will flood the mind if the preacher tackles this particular slant of the pericope.

Third, the relationship to Elisha demonstrates the endless line of splendor in which not only prophets, but all God's people stand. Elisha picks up the unfinished work of Elijah and continues in his train. Such a theme goes all the way from the mundane but necessary advice of how to succeed another minister to the lofty heights of the glorious continuity of the Hebrew-Christian tradition of which we are a part.

Finally, then, shifting from Elijah to Elisha we see the necessity of total commitment from the prophet. The parallels with the NT disciples are easily discernible here. The pictorial slaughtering of the oxen is the ancient symbol of cutting off the ties that would bind one in following devotedly the demands of God.

Second Lesson. Although the entire book of Galatians is concerned with freedom, this particular pericope could well be entitled, "The Christian's Declaration of Independence." Much of the previous study of the book in these Pentecost Sundays will be helpful to the minister in preparing individual sermons. Specifically, there are at least three areas worth exploring and developing homiletically. First, is the continuing theme of freedom in the epistle and especially in regard to the law. Though we have seen this idea continually in Galatians, it is still an important part of this passage. Paul's call to freedom and liberty obviously pertains to his continuing dialogue with the Judaizers over the law. We are to live by the Spirit, not by the law or flesh. For Paul, it is either *law* or *Christ* which saves, not both. Such a tension is still with the

Christian church and the preacher can immediately see the relevance of positing the spirit of Christ against the innumerable codes which many feel bring salvation.

The second important aspect of this passage is Paul's clear defense against the charges that liberty may produce license. Earlier we saw how he refutes this contention (Pentecost 4). Here he is more specific: "Though free from the law, Christians must not abuse their liberty" (notes, RSV, Oxford edition). The call to freedom is really a call to another kind of law—the law of love. Paul, as does Jesus, focuses this kind of law in neighbor love. Though this is reminiscent of Augustine's "Love God and do as you please," Paul is quite clear that this law of love places the Christian under specific responsibility.

This responsibility is the third theme of the pericope. In stating what the nature of love is he makes another contrast between law and love by showing the difference between flesh and Spirit. If one is led by the Spirit, he is no longer under law (flesh). Then, in a very specific way, he lists the works of the flesh which are not the acts of Christians hoping to inherit the kingdom of God. Then, in contrast, he lists the fruits of the Spirit which are the hallmarks of the Christian life. Such specific Christian traits should not only provide homiletical insight for the preacher, but should lay to rest those criticisms which avow that Christian liberty means license.

Gospel. The twin motifs in the Gospel lesson between commitment and discipleship are interesting parallels to the OT passage and provide the preacher with a background for sermon(s) on these two major subjects. First, Jesus' own commitment is before us as he prepared himself for the Jerusalem journey with all that connoted in terms of the unfolding of the last days of his ministry. There may be differences in considering how Jesus understood his mission at this particular time. Was there a messianic consciousness on his part? Or, as the Son of God did he already know the ending? Or, as one dedicated to the kingdom was he simply aware of its probable cost, leaving the sonship as a state to be certified only at his resurrection? Whatever may be the christological variations, the note of *commitment* is certain. The various translations emphasize the importance of Jesus' resolve: "he set his face," "he resolutely . . . ," "he firmly resolved." An interesting sermonic treatment awaits the development of this unflagging devotion to his message and mission. Without the necessity of suggesting emulation of Jesus, this full measure of devotion challenges our lives as "amiable" Christians.

Second, following the first, is the necessity of dedicated disciples. In the face of Jesus' own dedication, it is obvious that those who call him

Master and Lord will have stringent demands placed upon them. These claims of discipleship in vv. 57–62 which have parallels in the other Gospels are simply ways of stating the inevitable: single-minded devotion is demanded of those who would be disciples of Jesus. The preacher's perpetual task is to make this kind of a claim real to people whose devotion is simply elsewhere. How can a modern man be a disciple devoted to God's will in the midst of other claims? The answer to that question gives the modern preacher the most exciting challenge of his preaching. To put it another way, how can full commitment be interpreted in our day? To do this the preacher will need to do more than talk about Schweitzer. The modern work-a-day Christian needs to be shown not only that the call to commitment in these verses is relevant, he also needs to see that dedicated discipleship is directed to him as well.

The Seventh Sunday after Pentecost

Lutheran	*Roman Catholic*	*Episcopal*	*Presbyterian and UCC*
Isa. 66:10–14	Isa. 66:10–14	Isa. 66:10–14	Isa. 66:10–14
Gal. 6:1–10, 14–16	Gal. 6:14–18	Gal. 6:14–18	Gal. 6:11–18
Luke 10:1–9, 16	Luke 10:1–12, 17–20	Luke 10:1–9, 16–20	Luke 10:1–9

EXEGESIS

First Lesson: Isa. 66:10–14. The concluding chapters of Isaiah express a strong eschatological hope, a hope which looks to the Lord's power in the future. He will form a chosen remnant (65:7–9), which will enjoy the fullness of blessings (65:13–14). A new heaven and a new earth will be created (65:17–18) and a new harmony will prevail among men and in nature (65:19–25). Today's lesson continues this theme with a paean of joy over the new Jerusalem.

"Rejoice with Jerusalem" (v. 10): The dominant theme of joy is expressed in a triple command to rejoice: "rejoice" (*śimḥû*), used to express the emotion of joy; "be glad" (*gîlû*), literally, "shout in exultation" (cf. Isa. 9:3; Joel 2:21); "rejoice with her" (*śîśû*), literally, "display joy." In the following verses the new Jerusalem is compared to a mother who nourishes and comforts her children (cf. 2 Sam. 20:19; Isa. 54:1; Psalm 87; Ps. 131:2). The Lord promises (v. 12) prosperity "like a river." The association of the life-giving power of water and the favor of the Lord is strong in the OT (cf. Ezek. 47:8–12; Joel 3:18; Zech. 14:8). In vv. 12*b* and 13 the image shifts dramatically and now Yahweh is described as a mother who nurses, cares for, and comforts her children. Here, as in other places (Isa. 42:14; 49:15; 66:9), the dominant masculine imagery used for Yahweh yields to feminine imagery. The final verse (14) shifts from the imperative of v. 10 to the statement ("your heart shall rejoice") in describing the reaction upon "seeing" the new Jerusalem and knowing they are under the power ("hand") of the Lord.

The image of the eschatological Jerusalem, restored and fruitful, is powerful in exilic and postexilic writings (cf. Ezek. 37:24–28; Hag. 2:7; Zeph. 3:14–20; Zechariah 14) and in the NT appears as the heavenly Jerusalem (Gal. 4:24–31; Heb. 12:21; Rev. 21:1–22:5).

Second Lesson: Gal. 6:1–10, 14–16. The Second Lesson comes from two distinct parts of Galatians: 6:1–10, the continuation of the exhortation on the proper use of Christian freedom, and 6:14–18 where Paul, in his own hand, restates the essential theme of the letter. The content of 6:1–10 is a series of maxims for life in community (cf. Matthew 18), which serve as specifications of 5:14, and illustrations of the fruit of the Spirit (5:22–23). Paul writes dialectically, interspersing a series of exhortations with warnings. He exhorts the community to gentleness in fraternal correction (6:1, cf. Matt. 6:14–15; 18:15 ff.), compassion, and sharing of burdens (Rom. 15:1); sharing of goods with the catechists (cf. 1 Cor. 9:14; Phil. 4:15; Rom. 15:27); perseverance and courage, and love and care for all men. At the same time he cautions self-knowledge as an antidote to self-righteousness (cf. Matt. 7:1–5; 1 Cor. 11:28; 2 Cor. 13:5) and warns against self-deception. This list of practical directives shows that for Paul the "theological" problem of the letter is not abstracted from everyday life. Conflicts, divisions, lack of love and concern, self-righteousness, and domination are both the symptom and the effect of "perverting the Gospel" (1:7).

In the postscript Paul restates an essential point of the letter (6:12–13): compromise on the matter of circumcision is a yielding to flesh and would empty the cross of its saving power. Paul's boast (v. 14) is only in the cross (cf. 1 Cor. 2:2; 3:21; 2 Cor. 11:16; 12:9), "by which the world has been crucified," etc. "World" is a symbol of the powers allied against Christ. In almost mythical terms Paul attributes Christ's death to these powers (cf. 1 Cor. 2:6–8). They have, in effect, vented their fury in the crucifixion, and the resurrection is Christ's victory over them. Paul shares in this death and victory (Gal. 2:19–20; 5:24). In v. 15 Paul states that the result of Christian freedom is "a new creation" which is a new beginning and inner transformation of man. Consequent upon the new creation is a new rule or law for man (v. 16). The "Israel of God" is to walk in peace (right order and harmony between God and man; between man and man) and mercy (as recipients of God's mercy and exemplars of it in their lives).

Gospel: Luke 10:1–9, 16. After the proclamation of the conditions for discipleship (9:57–62), Luke collects sayings on the mission of the disciple under the instructions given to the seventy. The disciple is appointed and sent out (vv. 1, 3); he is to "go before" Jesus (v. 1), and to *re-present* him (v. 16). In what he does (the content, v. 9) and how he does it (the manner, vv. 3–7), the disciple is to imitate the Lord. By the use of the christological title (Lord, *Kyrios*), Luke addresses the words of Jesus to missionaries of his own time. "The harvest is plentiful" (v. 2): Harvest is often an eschatological image for the impending end (cf. Matt. 13:30). With the preaching of the kingdom (10:9) the seed is sown (8:4–8); now is the time of urgency for the mission. "As lambs in the midst of wolves": This is usually interpreted as an image of the disciples' defenselessness in the face of hostility. Another possibility is a reference to the eschatological prophecies of Isaiah (11:6, "The wolf shall dwell with the lamb," cf. Isa. 65:25), so that the mission of the seventy initiates the dawn of the new age. "Carry no purse," etc. (v. 4): Such action will be a sign of faith, of freedom from care, and of singleness of purpose (cf. Luke 22:35, the Last Supper, where Jesus recalls these words to the disciples). "On the road" (v. 4b): Again the road has the double meaning of journey and "way of discipleship." "Peace be to this house" (v. 5): Peace, here conceived dynamically like the word of God in the OT, is especially strong in Luke as a symbol of the salvation brought by Christ (1:79; 2:14, 29; 7:50; 8:48; 12:51; 19:38). Peace is characteristic of the harmony of the new age (cf. Gal. 6:16). "Eat what is set before you" (vv. 7, 8): Luke transmits this saying with an eye to the Gentile mission when the dietary laws will lose their force (cf. Acts 10:15).

"Heal the sick and say 'The Kingdom of God has come near to you' ": Just as in the ministry of Jesus the breaking in of God's rule or power is manifest in healing, so too will the disciple proclaim this power and manifest its presence. The *kingdom* is both the reign or rule of God, i.e., God calling man to the "obedience of faith" (Rom. 1:5), and also the realm or arena of life which man recognizes under God's power. "He who hears you, hears me" (v. 16): The character of the disciple as an authoritative representative of both Jesus and the one who "sent" Jesus is stressed. The words of Jesus on the lips of the disciple are powerful and lead men through Jesus to God.

HOMILETICAL INTERPRETATION

Many preachers may have a difficult time in discerning a unity in these particular lessons. One way to see them is to consider the coming of God's reign or kingdom as a link which binds them together. Though we normally think of the future in biblical faith as an eschatological term, the future need not be limited to "beyond the present age," but considered as a realized future—beyond the present moment to be sure— but attainable within the life span of the faithful. The Isaiah passage tells of the restoration of Jerusalem; in Galatians Paul writes of the Christian life in the new church; the Gospel relates the sending of the disciples to announce the nearness of the coming kingdom.

First Lesson. Previously (Pentecost 5) it was indicated that Jerusalem as a city is a viable theme for sermonic development both historically and metaphorically. Its history as the seat of temple worship for the Israelites, its part in the passion of Jesus Christ, and its continuing holy aura until the present day offer a theme for preaching. Not to be overlooked is the symbolic aspect of the city along with its figurative use. For example, it has had otherworldly connotations such as in the hymn, "Jerusalem the Golden."

> Jesus, in mercy bring us
> To that dear land of rest
> Who art, with God the Father
> And spirit, ever blest.

But Jerusalem also has been considered a very earthy and this-worldly metaphor. William Blake, the English poet, desired to see his homeland in figurative terms of a new Jerusalem:

> I will not cease from mental fight
> Nor shall my sword sleep in my hand
> Till we have built Jerusalem
> In England's green and pleasant land.

In the lesson for today, Jerusalem is personified as a woman—a mother who consoles her children. The preacher, without straining, may take the analogy and develop a theme that will be both creative and arresting.

Second Lesson. Paul ends the letter to the Galatians with specific admonitions for Christian living which make the charge against Pauline theology as being too doctrinal and abstract seem incredible. Further, the call to specific Christian behavior also absolves the apostle from the charge that Christian liberty frees one from moral responsibility or righteous living.

One way this passage can be treated sermonically is to lift up all of the marks of Christian living which Paul highlights in this pericope. For example, "take care of the one who fails" (v. 1); "bear one another's burdens" (v. 2); "whatever a man sows, he will reap" (v. 7); "let us do good to all men" (v. 10). Whether considered separately or together, these marks of the Christian life provide relevant material for the preacher.

Another approach would be to lift up other specific texts from the lesson to use as the focus of a sermon. Apart from those just considered, one could preach from a verse such as "And let us not grow weary in well-doing, for in due season we shall reap, if we do not lose heart." This familiar saying has eschatological connotations, to be sure, but it is also a necessary word to faithful Christians of any age who wonder if their labor is in vain.

The acme of the entire lesson is undoubtedly the last verses listed (vv. 14–16). In these Paul returns to his basic theme—indeed, his whole theology—and these two verses provide a text to reflect not only the message of this particular pericope, but the whole of Paul's thought. Three arresting thoughts are visible at once. 1. *Glory in the cross.* Other translations suggest "boast" for "glory." Paul moves here from the ethical life suggested above to the heart of his theology as the closing word to the Galatians. It is the crucifixion of Christ which overwhelms him and he can say confidently that he glories in the cross. The old hymn, "In the Cross of Christ I Glory," points up the ironical nature of the crucifixion:

> When the sun of bliss is beaming
> Light and love upon my way,
> From the cross the radiance streaming
> Adds more luster to the day.

This striking idea is followed closely by the second: 2. *The world is crucified to me and I to the world.* The elaboration of this tremendous concept leads to many fruitful possibilities as to what being crucified to the world means to us. 3. Finally, *the new creation.* Here is Paul's slogan for the new man in Christ. It is the summary not only of what the life in the Spirit is as over against the law, it is a veritable description of conversion. To be Christian is to be new and renewed.

Gospel. The commissioning of the disciples and sending them forth have parallels in the other Gospels as well as Luke. The comparison of these along with the variations in translations makes for a worthwhile sermonic approach. Specifically, however, the preacher may want to examine carefully the pericope before him. The mission of the seventy dramatizes both the nature of the disciples' labors and the words of advice given by the Master. In the first instance, they were forerunners preparing the way for Jesus much as John the Baptist had before them. Secondly, they learned from Jesus' departing words what discipleship would mean. They would be going into work where much was demanded, but few were available to do it. They would be poor, without possessions. They would heal the sick. These elements of discipleship may not have been attractive, but they were the price to be paid for their commitment to Christ. It doesn't take much imagination to see how we rationalize our own commitment as Christians away from the "hard sayings" of Jesus. In what way can the commissioning of the seventy be updated for our own commitment? We speak of the church in mission or the church as mission. Relating this specific pericope to the mission of the church in our day could result in a sermon both biblical and urgent.

Another important element in the lesson is the announcement of the coming of the kingdom. "The Kingdom of God has come near to you" (RSV). Historically, the kingdom has always had at least two elements— *present* and *future*. The kingdom has been referred to as future, meaning that it is beyond history. This belief has been dealt with under a variety of doctrines: last things, the coming of the parousia, the second coming, and eschatology. There is no doubt that this motif is in the NT. At the same time, it is equally clear that though the kingdom is a future reality, it is near at hand not only in the sense of eschatology but as a realizable possibility in the Christian's present. It is this belief that has been labeled "realized eschatology" meaning among other things that Jesus himself brought the kingdom into being with his coming. Such a view leads naturally into the idea of the kingdom being present. There are a host of instances to demonstrate that the kingdom is within one, grows like a seed, is in the midst of believers, and is near at hand. In this pericope the disciples are to announce that the kingdom is near, meaning that it is realizable in Jesus Christ. A sermon on the nature of the kingdom of God could arise naturally from this text.

The other intriguing note in this passage is the idea that the disciples speak for Jesus and he speaks for God. Thus, those who reject the disciples reject Jesus and ultimately God. This verse demonstrates the custodial quality of ministry and sacraments, the importance of the continuity of the church in history, and the persistence of the word of God into our own history.

The Eighth Sunday after Pentecost

Lutheran	*Roman Catholic*	*Episcopal*	*Presbyterian and UCC*
Deut. 30:9–14	Deut. 30:10–14	Deut. 30:10–14	Deut. 30:9–14
Col. 1:1–14	Col. 1:15–20	Col. 1:1–12	Col. 1:15–20
Luke 10:25–37	Luke 10:25–37	Luke 10:25–37	Luke 10:25–37

EXEGESIS

First Lesson: Deut. 30:9–14. The lesson today is from a liturgical address to the exilic community. In the Deuteronomic spirit there is a stress on the "return" in the double sense of "conversion" and return to the land of promise. V. 10 picks up the promise of v. 9 that the blessings of the Lord will be abundant, "if you obey the voice of the Lord." As in Greek, so in Hebrew the root of the verb "to obey" and "to hear" is the same, so that obedience is a radical or deep listening. "With all your heart and soul" (v. 10b): This is a favorite phrase in Deuteronomy, used to describe the totality and intensity with which man is to seek the Lord (4:29), love the Lord and walk according to his ways (6:5; 10:12; 11:13; 13:3; 26:16), obey him (30:2), and turn to him (30:10).

"The nearness of God's word" (vv. 11–14): Vv. 11 and 14 form a parenthesis stating the basic message which vv. 12–13 portray in metaphor. The Lord's revelation is not esoteric nor distant, for "the things that are revealed belong to us and to our children for ever" (20:29). "Is not too hard for you" (v. 11): The Hebrew word for "hard" carries also the nuance of wondrous or marvelous (cf. 1 John 5:3). In vv. 12 and 13 two comparisons are used to contrast the nearness of the Lord's commands to the inaccessibility of the heavens (the traditional "abode" of the divinity) and to the mysterious unknown of what lay beyond the sea, probably a reference to the Great Sea (the Mediterranean) which was a source of wonder to the Ancients. In Rom. 10:6–10 Paul uses the first of these images to describe the nearness of "the word of faith which we preach."

In the concluding verse the author again stresses the nearness of the word. "It is in your mouth": Man must express the word and presence of God. "It is in your heart": The word is to be a constant presence to man, "so that you can do it." Man must not simply hear; the word must be a presence to him; he must express it and act it out. This is, then, the ultimate meaning of "with all your heart and with all your soul" (30:10).

Second Lesson: Col. 1:1–14. As at Galatia, the community at Colossae was troubled by the activity of false teachers (2:8). These teachers rely on a superior knowledge (2:8, 18), prescribe worship of the "elemental spirits of the universe," angels, and other powers (2:8, 20). To this they join ascetical and ritual practices (2:16–23) which seem to be a mixture of Jewish and Gentile rites. Paul gives a twofold response to these teachers. In the doctrinal part of the letter (1:3–2:23) he proclaims the lordship of Christ over all the powers of the universe (2:15) and adapts to his purpose an early Christian hymn celebrating the primacy of Christ in creation and redemption (1:15–20). In the hortatory part (3:1–4:6) Paul urges a life "hid with Christ in God" (3:3), manifest not in ritual observance, but in love and harmony within the community (3:5–4:6). Aspects of the theology of the letter differ from the other Pauline letters. The *Christology* stresses not as much Christ's victory over sin, death, and the law, as over the cosmic powers. The *ecclesiology* portrays the church not simply as the local community (4:15), but as the worldwide "body of Christ" (1:18). Finally, the nearness of Christ's return has receded (cf. 1 Thess. 4:15–18 with Col. 3:4).

The letter begins with the usual greeting (1:1–2), followed by a long thanksgiving in vv. 3–8 (one sentence in Greek), a prayer for the community, vv. 9–12, and an introduction to the Christ hymn (vv. 13–14). Paul praises the community for its faith, love, and hope—a triad frequent in Paul (Rom. 5:1–5; 12:3–9; 1 Cor. 13:13; 1 Thess. 5:8; Eph. 1:15–18). Hope, which is strong in this letter (1:5, 23, 27), is a trust in God's promises (Rom. 4:18). It shapes present attitudes (1 Cor. 13:7) but is directed to future fulfillment. Since the false teachers try to impose different experiences on the community, Paul concludes the thanksgiving (vv. 6–8) by appealing to their experience of life "bearing fruit" according to the true gospel, which they have received from an authenticated minister.

Paul then adds his prayer for the church. The striking parallels between the prayer and the thanksgiving are a subtle way of urging the community to persevere in the life they have been living. In this prayer Paul asks that the community obtain the very things the opponents claim as their prerogatives—knowledge and power. In v. 12 Paul urges thanksgiving for the gifts received ("share in the inheritance") of liberation (cf. Rom. 3:24; 8:23) and forgiveness of sin, granted by the Father in Christ. By this petition a transition is made from the picture of the work of God in Christ, found in the other letters, to the more comprehensive Christology of the hymn (1:15–20).

Gospel: Luke 10:25–37. The passage begins with a question (vv. 25–29). Here Luke alters his source (cf. Mark 12:28–31; Matt. 22:34–40) in two important respects. The question in Luke is about "eternal life"

and in citing the OT (Deut. 6:5; Lev. 19:18), Luke omits the word
"second" in describing the commands to love God and neighbor. For
Luke the great commandment is a unity with a double focus. The unity
is love and on this hinges eternal life (cf. 1 John 4:16).

The parable (vv. 30–35) is not really an answer to the lawyer's question. The real point of the parable is in the surprising goodness of the
Samaritan. The lawyer asks how to identify the neighbor *whom* he must
love and finds what it means to be a neighbor *who* loves. The shock and
surprise of the parable come in locating the higher law of love in the
Samaritan. *The situation* (v. 30): A man is robbed, stripped, and left half
dead. He is thus deprived of all identity. The passersby see him not as
Jew or Samaritan, not as well known or unknown, but only as one in
need. *The failure of the priest and Levite* (v. 31): Caution should be
observed against reading an anticlerical polemic into their neglect. If
the injured man were in fact dead, contact with him would have brought
ritual defilement (Lev. 21:1–4; Num. 19:11–16). The drama of the
parable comes in the conflict of two laws, the law of prescribed duty and
the law of love. *The action of the Samaritan* (vv. 33–35): All three who
travel the road "see" the injured man; only the Samaritan, when he saw,
had compassion. This term is used by Luke to describe God's love for
man (1:78), the care of Jesus for the widow (7:13), and the reaction of
the father to the prodigal (15:20). Compassion is the bridge between
mere seeing and action. The details of v. 34 characterize the personal
investment of the Samaritan. The payment of the innkeeper, v. 35, often
considered an afterthought, is crucial to the parable. By the law of that
time, a person in debt to another could be enslaved until payment of the
debt (cf. Matt. 18:28–30). By paying in advance the Samaritan has thus
not only cared for the man in need, but assures his future freedom.

The lawyer's admission in v. 37 that the one who "showed mercy" is
the neighbor, may be an allusion to Hos. 6:6, "I desire steadfast love
[*hesed*, also translated "mercy"] and not sacrifice," confirming that the
point of the parable is the higher law of love. Like that of the prodigal
son, this parable is a gospel within a Gospel, a parable ultimately of
God's surprising, shocking, and liberating love for man manifest in the
event of Jesus.

HOMILETICAL INTERPRETATION

Two intriguing themes come out of these lessons today, either of
which could embrace creative preaching. One, the thread of *covenant* in
one way or another runs through all the pericopes. In Deuteronomy there
is a contrast between the tablets of law and the new covenant within the

hearts of the people. For Paul, the new covenant is in Christ who freed us from the law. In Luke, Jesus answers the lawyer by going beyond the legal demands to a compassionate story of neighbor love. Second, there could be an interesting examination of the nature of *word*. In the OT the word is near: in mouth, heart, etc. In Colossians, the gospel is the word of truth. And, in the Gospel, the good Samaritan story was a word which went beyond the written word of the law.

First Lesson. In the Deuteronomic story God continues his lover's quarrel with his people Israel. We see clearly the two motifs mentioned above. He is once again reminding the people of their covenant with him, a covenant made and broken and always renewable. This time, in contrast with the covenant inscribed on the tablets of stone, the covenant is not far off, mysterious, or lofty. It is closer than hands or feet; it is within. These verses are reminiscent of Jer. 31:31–33 where God affirms that the new covenant will place the law within—written upon their hearts. In the First Lesson, the people learn that if they repent and turn to God they will find that the commandment is also within.

The second theme may not be as discernible, but certainly is as arresting. The RSV and JB emphasize in v. 14 that the commandment is a *word* that is very near to you. The notes in the latter version make clear that this concept is the theology of the word associated with wisdom literature, culminating in the prologue to the Fourth Gospel, and used by Paul as the word of faith. This can be a significant idea for preaching since it has several facets that are at the heart of Christian faith: 1. the word is at the center of revelation; 2. the doctrine of the word as usually associated with the Reformation; 3. the current word-event theology; and 4. the correlation of the word of God with the communicator's concern for speech as the basic sensorium of communication. Any or all of these are important in dramatizing how God has spoken—and continues to speak—through the Bible and the church to his people.

Second Lesson. The salutation or introduction to the letter to the Colossians provides a myriad of preachable ideas. We have previously mentioned the word of God which in this letter is equated with the word of truth or the gospel. There are other themes equally important. One is the astounding affirmative tone of the letter. Paul, writing from prison, is greeting the church at Colossae in a most positive manner born out of a deep faith, not a shallow optimism. Their faith, too, must have been of the same kind even though he was writing to correct some specious teachings. However, it is his method of addressing those in the household of faith that commands our attention and should commend itself to our own ways of dealing with one another. So much of the gospel—even in preaching—is presented as judgmental, negative, scolding, and depressing. Paul calls them "faithful," thanking God for them, for their faith and their love. What a difference would occur in the church's outreach if the gospel message could be thought of more in the affirmative key—a note of buoyant faith even in adversity.

Another striking thought is the discovery in vv. 4–5 of the familiar Pauline triad of faith, hope, and love. The more familiar text is from the thirteenth verse of the thirteenth chapter of 1 Corinthians: "So faith, hope, love abide these three; but the greatest of these is love." The combination of these texts along with other similar ones in Paul makes a worthwhile approach for a vital sermon theme.

An exciting sermon theme in the pericope may well be the idea of *saints* in this passage. In the RSV the term is used three times and seemingly in three different ways: 1. v. 2 gives Paul's greetings to the church at Colossae; the members are addressed as "saints and faithful brethren"; 2. v. 4 suggests the Colossians have love "for all the saints"; 3. v. 12 indicates that Paul and the Colossians are both qualified "to share in the inheritance of the saints in light." Though the usage in the third instance may refer to life after death, those addressed in the first two cases are certainly living Christians. This is borne out in other translations where saints are referred to as "holy ones" (NAB) and "God's people" (NEB). The notes in the JB point out that the term refers to Christians either called to live the life of light here on earth or it can be used eschatologically. The NAB suggests more strongly the present use of the term when it affirms that the term denotes members of the Christian community much as the OT usage of the phrase "people of God." The sermonic possibilities burgeon when one begins to ponder the relevance of relating that term to faithful Christians, ordinary folk who are called to be extraordinary. To see the term as a description of God's people makes us all aware of our responsibility to be faithful. We cannot bask in the warmth of the great figures of the church—living or dead. We, too, are called to be saints—holy ones, God's people.

Gospel. The major problem in preaching from the Gospel lesson is that it is too familiar. Surely every preacher in Christendom has a sermon on the good Samaritan. To come to an old pericope with fresh eyes takes an effort, but it is worth the work. First of all, a new exegesis of the passage brings different insights. For example, as the exegesis shows, neighbor love confers freedom and liberation as well as concern.

One creative approach to appropriating the Gospel through the lesson is to focus on one or more of the personages in the pericope. Take the lawyer, for example. Presumably he was a learned and religious man. He knew the *Shema*, the daily Jewish prayer, but he wanted to test the limits of his religious duty so he asked his question. He may have wanted to trap Jesus, put him to the test, or as other translations suggest "disconcert him" (JB) and "pose him this problem" (NAB). In any event, he knew what was right but it wasn't clear that he could go beyond affirmation to participation. Jesus' telling of the story forced him to see participation as a decisive element of Christian love. The method of storytelling did two things: 1. it let the lawyer convict himself; the method is similar to the one Nathan used with David (cf. Pentecost 4: exegesis of First Lesson); 2. it took the argument out of the realm of the rational and placed it in the existential.

Other characters in the story lend themselves to the same kind of treatment. We often mention the Samaritan in our sermons. To make him terribly real to us we would have to translate that term as the most despicable outcast of all society. In that day the Samaritan was an alien and a heretic. What would he be called today? The priest and Levite may seem obvious when viewed historically, but when examined in our present day how would these figures be characterized so the modern-day congregation would be involved? Or, perhaps the most startling of all: could the Gospel take on a new meaning if we could see ourselves as the victim? To see ourselves as the one needing the help, seeking the aid, and receiving the succor might take us out of the realm of the ordinary and lift us into an existence where grace could be vitally grasped.

The Ninth Sunday after Pentecost

Lutheran	*Roman Catholic*	*Episcopal*	*Presbyterian and UCC*
Prov. 8:22–35	Gen. 18:1–10a	Gen. 18:1–10a	Gen. 18:1–10a
Col. 1:21–28	Col. 1:24–28	Col. 1:21–28	Col. 1:24–28
Luke 10:38–42	Luke 10:38–42	Luke 10:38–42	Luke 10:38–42

EXEGESIS

First Lesson: Prov. 8:22–35 (Lutheran cycle). This is the second discourse in Proverbs where personified wisdom speaks (1:20–33; 8:1–36). In the OT wisdom is identified with the word of God, the law (Sir. 24:23), and the spirit, and, in the later books, personified wisdom appears with prophetic, divine, and messianic traits, though standing apart from God.

Today's lesson describes the origin of wisdom (vv. 22–26), her role in creation (vv. 26–31), and exhorts man to seek wisdom (32–36). Wisdom is the decisive act or law in which the meaning of creation is disclosed. In personifying wisdom and in assigning it a role in creation, the OT paves the way for Christ as "the wisdom of God" (1 Cor. 1:24). The language describing the quest for wisdom uses images of listening and watching. Like Mary in the Gospel reading, man is to sit before wisdom, watch, and listen, and thus he will find favor and life.

First Lesson: Gen. 18:1–10a (Roman Catholic, Episcopal, and Presbyterian cycles). This lesson contains the Yahwist account of the Lord's appearance to Abraham to confirm the promise of an heir. There is some confusion in this old narrative. In 18:1 Yahweh appears; then three visitors appear, 18:2–9, and Yahweh reappears in 18:10. We find here the common motif of ancient sagas that gods appear in disguise to men (cf. Genesis 19; Tob. 5:1–21). The point of the narrative is in the surprising character of divine events and the human dimension of how man accepts the promise and presence of God. In v. 1 Abraham is at his tent, in the heat of the day when visitors would normally not be expected. As the story unfolds Abraham busily extends hospitality to the unexpected guests and the story ends with the renewed promise to Abraham (cf. Gen. 12:2; 13:15–16; 15:2–15; 17:15–21). The connection with the Gospel may be in the surprising quality of God's presence and in the picture of Abraham as a combination of Martha (v. 6, "Abraham hastened") and of Mary (Abraham stands in silence while his guests eat, v. 8). Abraham emerges as a model of both service and patience.

Second Lesson: Col. 1:21–28. Having affirmed the universal lordship of Christ and the reconciliation of all things through him (1:15–20), Paul now applies this general teaching to the Colossians. He contrasts their previous Gentile state (estrangement and enmity, v. 21) with what God has done in Christ. "He has reconciled" (v. 22): The root of this verb is the same as the verb "to change or exchange," so Paul is talking about a radical new status the Christian has been given—the change from enmity to acceptance. "In the body of his flesh by his death" (v. 22): This is a reference to the crucifixion, but the terminology may also mirror Jewish "day of atonement" theology where every reconciliation is sealed by a death. "In order to present you," etc. (vv. 22–23): Paul looks to both the present and the future. The Christian is now blameless and is to remain so by not "shifting from the hope of the gospel." Again Paul joins the indicative (what God has done in Christ) with an imperative (what man is to do in response to this gift).

Introduction to polemical part, vv. 24–29. Having described himself as a minister of the gospel (v. 23), Paul recounts his own experience of discipleship and its demands, thus making an implicit contrast between his ministry and the boasting and "philosophy" of the opponents (2:8, 23). Paul rejoices in his sufferings (Rom. 5:3; 2 Cor. 11:30; 12:9; Phil. 2:17; 3:7–10), and he completes what is lacking in Christ's afflictions. By this statement Paul is not assigning any inadequacy to the reconciliation effected by God in Christ. He is describing the demands of the Christian ministry "for the sake of his body, the church." He also uses the apocalyptic motif that sufferings are the prelude to final glory. A second apocalyptic motif is found in the word of God described as "the mystery hidden for ages and generations, but now made manifest" (v. 26). The idea of God's secret plan which will be revealed in the end time is strong in Jewish apocalyptic. Paul "demystifies" this idea by locating the plan in the gospel he proclaims, "the glory of this mystery, which is Christ in you" (v. 27). Thus, in the polemical context of the letter, Paul affirms the true nature of Christian mystery. It is not esoteric speculation or adherence to ritual practices, but hearing what God has done in Christ, the true Christian wisdom (v. 28). The real "mystery" of the Christian life is the tension between the "already"—the realization of what God has done in Christ and of Christ's universal lordship—and the "not yet" —the fact that the effects of this lordship are not visible, but that the Christian lives with his life "hid with Christ in God" (3:3).

Gospel: Luke 10:38–42. Today's Gospel follows the parable of the good Samaritan. At first glance there seems to be little connection between the two pericopes. However, since Luke brackets both narratives by references to Jesus at prayer (10:21–24; 11:1–2), it seems that he saw a connection between the two. As the exegesis will indicate, both narratives are illustrations of the "great commandment" (10:27). In one case this commandment is lived out in selfless care, attention, and devotion to a neighbor; in the second, by a singleminded devotion to and presence before the Lord (Mary's action). The story of Martha and Mary has many of the characteristics of a parable. The vivid portrayal of the situation (Martha bustling with the meal preparations, Mary at the feet of Jesus) engages the reader's attention. There is a "surprise" in the words of Jesus (vv. 41–42). Having just read the parable of the Samaritan, one would expect Jesus to urge Mary to help her sister. This story could well be called "an acted parable." (Cf. Luke 13:6 ff., the parable of the fig tree, and Mark 11:12–14, the cursing of the fig tree.)

The setting (vv. 38–39): The love of Jesus for this family is well attested in the NT (cf. John 11; 12:1–8). "Mary, who sat at the Lord's feet": This is a technical term for a disciple learning from a rabbi (Acts 22:3), as well as a position of supplication (Luke 7:38), of repose (Luke 8:35), and of thanksgiving (Luke 17:16). *Martha's complaint:* Martha is described as distracted. Literally the verb means "drawn away" and in later Christian literature becomes a technical term for the cares of the world which draw a person from God. *Jesus' answer* (vv. 41–42): Jesus gives a twofold answer. Martha is chided for being "anxious and troubled." The word for anxious (*merimnas*) is used frequently in the NT for the cares of the world. In Luke 8:14 the thorns which choke the growth of the seed are cares, and in the teaching on discipleship in Luke 12, anxiety is an attitude in opposition to trust. Not Martha's actions (service) are chided, but her attitude.

Much effort has been expended in invoking this saying of Jesus in favor of "contemplation" over action. Such exegesis is atomistic. In the total Lucan context we have a completion of the command to love God and neighbor. Care and love are shown equally in action for neighbor and a silent attentiveness before the Lord. Both the presence of the Christian before the Lord and the manifestation of this presence by love of neighbor are equally important in Luke for the way of discipleship.

HOMILETICAL INTERPRETATION

The lessons for this Sunday bring together in two of the pericopes one of the important themes in biblical literature—the personification of wisdom. The First and Second Lessons seem to be in stark contrast to the familiar little vignette of Mary and Martha. In Proverbs, wisdom is spoken of as an agent of divine creation, in Colossians Jesus Christ has become the personification of the mystery hidden for generations. The Mary and Martha story is not nearly so lofty, but they all three revolve around the centrality of the divine: in creation, in Christ, in his word.

First Lesson. The passage from Proverbs is at once challenging and perilous. It is difficult, for the concept of wisdom in relation to the creative work of God as a divine agent and preexistent reality is fraught with abstractness. On the other hand, the pericope opens up a fruitful approach to the doctrine of creation and the divine planning back of the universe. This lesson is reminiscent of other familiar ones in the Bible and will lead the preacher into several books as he develops his preaching. For example, the creation stories in Genesis would be one. Then Psalm 139, with its emphasis upon the omnipotence, omniscience, and omnipresence of God, could be related to the Proverbs passage. In addition, Job 38 is a majestic accompaniment to the theme of the present passage. Finally, the NT refers to Jesus himself as the wisdom of God (1 Cor. 1:24). We see this idea in Colossians and, of course, in the first chapter of John's gospel. There the concept is referred to as the *Logos*, but it is of the same nature as the wisdom concept in the OT and contains ample material for themes on God's divine activity in creation.

Two other ideas, though possibly subsidiary, are nevertheless important. One is focused in vv. 30–31, ". . . then I was beside him, like a master workman; and I was daily his delight, rejoicing before him always, rejoicing in his inhabited world and delighting in the sons of men." The idea of humor, playfulness, joy, and laughter has always intrigued persons in regard to religion. These verses could open up this interesting idea. The other translations give credence to the same thing. One suggests "ever at play in his presence, at play everywhere in his world" (JB). What would it mean to be playful in the presence of the holy? Reinhold Niebuhr and Harvey Cox, to name only two, have written helpfully on this idea.

Second Lesson. In the Second Lesson at least four major notions command the preacher's attention. First, Paul reminds the Colossians of their history of salvation (*Heilsgeschichte*). He reminds them they were pagans —estranged and evil—but Christ reconciled them through his death. Now they are holy and blameless if they remain steadfast in the faith. This remembering of one's salvation history which is so much a part of the Pauline corpus of writing is a helpful contemporary word to Christians who continually need to hear the good news of what God through Christ has done for them. In a sense, this is the telling of the old, old story.

The second motif is Paul's surprising comment that he rejoices in his suffering. We know that Paul wrote this letter from jail and since he had not seen these people personally the writing takes on even more poignancy. It should be clear that Paul was not seeking suffering in order to gain more spiritual rewards. He simply was recounting the price he had to pay for bringing the gospel to the pagan world and accepted gladly that dimension of his discipleship. It seems strange to modern Christians to hear terms such as rejoicing in suffering or being happy or joyful to suffer for another, especially when the cost of discipleship for most Christians is so cheap. The Bonhoeffers and Schweitzers are the exceptions in our day; what Paul was describing was the accepted norm for discipleship in the early church. One other thought is connected with this suffering of Paul's. It was not an individual stoicism for personal salvation; it was suffering for the sake of Christ's body which Paul clearly labels the *church*.

The third idea in this pericope continues the earlier theme of *mystery*. Paul speaks of mystery in several places in his writings, and, as we have seen, this concept ties in with the personification of wisdom in the Proverbs passage and the *Logos* in the Johannine writings. In this pericope Paul defines exactly what he means by the mystery or rather he solves the mystery: "The secret is this": it is Christ in you, the hope of glory. What was mysterious from the foundations of the world is now made clear in Christ Jesus. The word of God is fully known. That intriguing idea is still arresting: Christ in you, the hope of glory.

The fourth concept is not unlike the above, but the emphasis is upon Paul's desire to "present every man mature in Christ" (1:28, RSV). One of the most modern concerns in our psychological age is to achieve maturity. It is of more than passing interest that this term is used in certain translations of Pauline thought to express what he meant by the goal of his labors in behalf of others. Though the word "perfect" is also used, the term has contemporary force when seen as "mature" or "complete." As is indicated in Philippians, "pressing on toward the goal for the prize of the upward call of God in Christ Jesus" is a sign of mature-mindedness. That upward call is still good news.

Gospel. The brief encounter of Jesus with Martha and Mary is a warm human interest story whose earthy details often obscure the main point. Much can be made of the homey details of one sister who was obviously concerned to minister to the needs of the Master while the other was content to sit at his feet. The focusing on the sisters' personalities has limited value. As in most of the stories in the gospel, there is a point and in this one the fulcrum of the text is: "one thing is needful" (RSV). It seems clear that Mary was being rewarded for paying heed to Jesus' teachings and listening "to the Word of God" (notes in JB). From our side of the resurrection this one thing necessary would take on a different dimension, but certainly not a completely different thought. If for Mary the one thing needful was to pay heed to Jesus, or to listen to God's word, it is obvious that for us the one thing needful is also to pay heed to Jesus who himself becomes God's word.

The other arresting idea is suggested in the exegesis where we are reminded that Luke bracketed the good Samaritan story with the Mary and Martha incident. Together they illustrate the great commandment (10:27) to love God and neighbor. In reverse order, Mary's attitude illustrates the former and the good Samaritan confirms the second. Such an insight provides the basis for an interesting sermon on the great commandment illustrated by these two familiar stories. Being attentive to the Lord—the one thing needful— and the love of neighbor are not two different and contrasting ideas. They are two facets of the *one* gospel.